the ctc guide to
family cycling

PUBLISHED BY JAMES PEMBROKE PUBLISHING
90 WALCOT STREET, BATH, BA1 5BG, UK
Tel: 01225 337777
Email: jamesp@jppublishing.co.uk
Website: www.jppublishing.co.uk

© Dan Joyce & James Pembroke Publishing 2008

Text: Dan Joyce
Images: Jason Patient, Steve Behr/Stockfile,
iStockPhoto.com, Dan Joyce, Sue Darlow, Martin
Breschinski, Carlton Reid, Andy Shrimpton, Seb
Rogers, Adam Coffman, Peter Eland, Steve Melia,
Brian Walker, David Dansky, and cycle companies
as captioned. Cover photo by Fotosearch
Design: James Houston, Will Slater & Neil Smith

Printed and bound in Slovakia by MKT Print

A catalogue record for this book is available from
the British Library.

ISBN: 978-0-9548176-4-0

ACKNOWLEDGMENTS:
To CTC national office staff, in particular Chris Juden
of the Technical Department and everyone in the
Training Department, for their valuable advice.

CTC is the UK's largest cycling membership
organisation with 70,000 members and affiliates.
To join CTC, or to find out more, turn to the
Resources section on page 188.

Note:
Prices and distributors change. Web links die.
Products recommended in this book are excellent
examples of what to look for, but we can't guarantee
ongoing availability.

The cycle industry still uses both imperial and
metric measurements.

Contents

66

the ctc guide to
family cycling

working for cycling

▶ For more about CTC, please visit:
www.ctc.org.uk

132

1.1

On your bikes!

THIS IS A BOOK about getting children on bikes, from babes in arms to teenagers and all points in between. It tells you what you need to buy and how to use it. It's aimed at two groups of people: families who have, or are about to buy, bicycles; and keen cyclists who have, or are about to have, families.

Cycling is an activity the whole family can enjoy. Many families already do so, as a trip to a railway cycle route on a summer weekend will reveal. You'll see family groups pedalling along at their own pace, heading for a picnic or a pub lunch. Younger children love this. It's time spent with family, talking together, discovering things, and enjoying fresh air and exercise. It's a fine way to spend an August Sunday, and a good introduction to recreational cycling.

However, the scope of cycling is much wider than this. You can do the school run by bike. You can scorch along a forest track with your 12-year-old, weaving between the trees like the speeder-bikes from *Return of the Jedi*. You can go on holiday by bike, cycling from one French campsite to another. Whatever the journey, within reason, a bike can take you there.

BIKES FOR ALL

Cycling is very egalitarian. Almost everyone is capable of learning to ride a bicycle (or, if not, a tricycle) and most British adults can readily afford to buy and run one. As a result there are more than 20 million bicycles in the UK, with one in three adults owning at least one. Among children aged 6-16 cycling is the second most popular physical activity, just after swimming and ahead of football.

While cycling is a fantastic form of recreation and transport in later life, for a child it has an even more significant role. It's the only form of transport where a child is not just a passenger. For a child old enough to make his or her own journeys, it's a huge boost to independence.

The freedom that a bike brings, and the greater speed and exhilaration involved compared to being on foot, means that learning to ride one is a milestone in a child's life. Most children can't wait to crack the magic skill of balancing a two-wheeler. Once you have learned to ride a bike, then – proverbially – you never forget.

Cast your mind back to your own childhood, where summer days seemed to stretch ahead forever. Now try to imagine those days without your bike. It's impossible. Cycling permeated our lives, whether we were scrambling over scrubland or popping wheelies in the park – where there really were jumpers for goalposts.

Children's cycling today is more circumscribed, mostly due to parental fears of traffic and strangers. Yet children still like riding bikes. They just need the opportunity, the right equipment and the necessary skills. You can give them that.

You can't force children to become enthusiastic cyclists, but if you give

Cycling is ideal exercise for children. It's fun, it's free, it requires no special facilities, and it can be incorporated into their daily routine
Photo: istock

them the right bike and enough chances to use it you won't have to: ultimately, cycling sells itself.

THE HEALTHY OPTION

Cycling is so good for you and your children that doctors do indeed recommend it. Since 1992, the British Medical Association has urged the Government to do more to encourage cycling so that the population as a whole gets on its collective bike. Why? Because it's preventative medicine for a variety of 21st century ills, the big ones of which are coronary heart disease and obesity.

Western society is increasingly sedentary, particularly children, who end up being ferried everywhere in the family car. We are creating, as one academic put it, a nation of battery-reared children instead of free-range children.

The prescription? Better school dinners are only a small part of the equation. It's not just about cutting down on junk food, although that helps. Children in ages past used to eat bread and dripping sandwiches. What's different today is not so much the rise in calories consumed but the fall in calories expended. Kids just aren't active enough.

Health experts recommend that children take an hour or more of moderate exercise per day, and adults half an hour. Cycling is perfect because it's an aerobic exercise that's easy to incorporate into the daily routine. You can't swim to school or play tennis all the way to the cinema. You can easily go by bike.

Cycling uses the biggest muscles in the body. It burns around 300 calories per hour at an easy pace, up to around 700 or more for strenuous mountain biking. Even at a moderate pace, you need only cycle for half an hour each day to burn 11lb of fat over the course of a year, given no other lifestyle changes. That half an hour a day is enough to halve your risk of heart disease and improve overall health – so much so that regular adult cyclists enjoy a fitness level equivalent to someone 10 years younger.

Walking is good too, but cycling takes you four times as far for the same effort. It is, in fact, the most efficient form of muscle-powered locomotion on the planet. Those racehorses rippling over the grass of the derby's final furlong burn energy like a steam engine burns coal compared to the efficient grace of you pedalling your bicycle.

It won't always feel that easy if you're coming back to cycling after a long lay-off. Minor aches in the thighs, calves and buttocks are common as your body gets used to being on a bike. But no bike should be persistently uncomfortable. If it is, it's the wrong bike or wrongly set up – keep reading!

Cycling is even good for your mental well-being. Like other forms of aerobic exercise you get a 'lift' afterwards, which may be due to the release of endorphins. Several studies have suggested that exercise helps adult participants deal with stress better. What about children? I can't offer you data but, as a parent, it's questionable whether you need it: you can instantly see the difference in behaviour between a child who has had fresh air and exercise and one who hasn't.

THE GREEN MACHINE

As a bicycle burns only calories, it minimises your carbon footprint. The more you use it instead of other forms of transport, the more you help fight global warming – which will have a bigger impact in your children's lives than your own.

Cycling is better for the local environment, too. It reduces traffic on the roads – one fifth of which is due to the school run on weekdays – and so combats congestion. It reduces noise. It reduces the double-parking and driver frustration that can cause accidents near school gates.

Cycling's environmental and health benefits don't require any sacrifices either. In fact, the opposite is true. Cycling is much cheaper and, over short distances, faster. It's the tortoise to the car's hare. A car capable of 60mph will spend much of its time at 0mph in a traffic jam or going nowhere in search of a parking space. A bicycle will take you door to door at 10-15mph in almost any traffic conditions – or by avoiding the traffic entirely through

Learning to ride a bike is a real milestone in the life of any child
Photo: istock

a combination of backstreets and cycleways. With few delays and no late arrivals, journey times are predictable by bike. And if you are running late, you can literally step on it.

You might not want to ride if you've far to go – perhaps your job is in the next town, or you need to make a triangular journey via the nursery. Most journeys aren't far. The bulk of UK journeys are under two miles, which is just enough to put a healthy glow in your cheeks if you're cycling. According to the Department for Transport's latest National Travel Survey, the average distance for all journeys is only 6.9 miles, which is just half an hour or so by bike.

Savings will soon start to stack up, leaving more of the family budget that can be spent elsewhere. The only fuel costs are the cornflakes you would have eaten anyway, instead of a pound a litre at the petrol pump. Cycle often enough and you could save £1,000 a year in petrol alone, before factoring in parking and other charges.

In rural situations, cycling is seldom faster than other transport but it is more pleasant. You're out in the fresh air, in surround-sound countryside, travelling fast enough to cover a mile in minutes but slow enough not to miss anything. Because you travel so quietly, you get a more intimate view of nature. It's like going for a country walk with the added benefit that you get somewhere at the same time.

GREAT ESCAPES
Getting on a bicycle gives you back a sense of freedom that's sometimes lost in busy 21st-century lives. Cycling home lets you work through problems en route rather than bringing them through the door. Cycling together to the seaside one summer's day can give a sense of adventure and achievement that will never be lost.

Many of the experiences children have today are essentially passive. On a bike they're back in control, making things happen, finding out what they're capable of. And it will make them healthy as well as happy.

You don't need much to get a huge amount out of cycling: just the right bikes, the right equipment, and a few pointers. It's all here.

The right bike

IN REAL TERMS, bicycles are more affordable today than they have ever been. That doesn't mean they're cheap, and the catalogue-shop 'bargain' that costs £99 will likely be more trouble than it's worth. It will be heavy and equipped with clunky components that barely work – slipshod gears or brakes, or suspension that sags like a punctured football. A bike like this is sometimes referred to in the trade as a BSO: a Bicycle-Shaped Object.

This isn't snobbery, rather a recognition of the fact that a decent bicycle that you can use regularly rather than once in a blue moon will cost from around £200 when bought new. Bikes aren't toys. They cost the same kind of money as desktop computers, with the same implications when it comes to value versus performance.

The less you're going to spend, the more you need to remember this maxim: less is more. It's invariably better to buy something that's simple and that works properly rather than wasting money on something complicated that doesn't.

The more a bike's manufacturing budget is diluted by fashionable 'must have' extras, the more corners will be cut to bring the bike in on budget, and so the worse it will ultimately be. A £200 bike that has front and rear suspension and a set of disc brakes will be awful; a £200 bike that has V-brakes and no suspension at all could be great.

Bargains do exist. But generally, as with most things, you get what you pay for.

SIZE MATTERS

Your bike has to be the right size for you, just like a pair of shoes. Otherwise it will make cycling awkward and uncomfortable. There are simple adjustments that you can make to a bike to make it fit you better (see Chapter 9) but it needs to be broadly the right size to begin with. For that reason, don't be tempted by any bike that's too big or small, even if it is a bargain. Shop at a proper bike shop where you can try bikes for size.

Bikes are traditionally sized on the frame's seat-tube length. Comparisons can be tricky, however, because of compact frames and different methods of measuring. A more reliable method for finding the right size bike is based on the fact that the medium-sized model in almost every bike range is one designed to fit the average-height man.

This makes sense when you think about it. Manufacturers want to sell as many bikes as possible and they'll do that by making their bike range fit the majority of the population.

The average British man is 5ft 9in or 175.5cm. The bike that will fit Mr

An urban mountain bike is a versatile all-rounder that suits tarmac roads and gentler off-road tracks
Photo: Ridgeback Cyclone, from Madison, a division of H Young (Operations) Limited

Average is the average frame size – the arithmetic mean. If the bike comes in 50-58cm sizes, for example, then it's the 54cm model. If it comes in 16, 18 or 20in, it's 18in.

If you're taller or shorter than Mr Average, halve the difference and add (taller) or subtract (shorter) from the medium bike size. That's the bike that should fit you. So in the above examples, if you're 180cm – about 4cm bigger than average – you want the 56cm frame; if you're 5ft 5in, you want the 16in frame.

If you fall between sizes, try the ones either side and see what feels best. See also Chapter 9 for the adjustments you can make to tweak the fit.

WHAT TO LOOK FOR

Again, bikes are like shoes: there are different types for different occasions. Mountain bikes are the most popular, but they're not always the best option, in the same way that hiking boots aren't always the ideal footwear.

Whatever type of bike you choose, there are additional considerations if you're going to be using that bike to carry or tow children. Firstly, gears. It doesn't much matter how many your bike has but they must go low enough. Even small children are heavy, as anyone who has carried a baby in a papoose will know. On flat roads the extra weight isn't a big issue but you will feel it on even the slightest

A hardtail mountain bike can be used for solo off-road riding as well as family cycling. You'll need frame eyelets to fit a rear rack
Photo: Trek 4500, from Trek Bicycle Corp

gradient. Live on a hill? Get a bike with a triple chainset. Brakes need to be powerful so that you can slow down your heavier and more preciously-loaded bike reliably and quickly.

This is as much a matter of correct set-up and brake quality as it is brake type. Disc brakes, drum brakes, V-brakes, cantilever brakes – all are fine. Even sidepull brakes can work okay. Old-fashioned rod-brakes look cute but function abysmally.

Wider handlebars give you more leverage for steering a steady course when you're riding with a child seat or trailer cycle. Child seats skew the weight distribution on the bike, while trailer cycles can exert a 'tail wags dog' effect. Having your hands a bit wider apart helps compensate.

Your bike will need threaded frame eyelets to fix a rear carrier rack onto it if you want to use a rack-mounted child seat or trailer cycle. If you want to use a child seat that clamps to the seat tube (and possibly seat stays too), you should avoid expensive and superlight frame materials that could crimp or fracture under the clamps; sturdy steel or more basic aluminium tubing is safer.

Consider how much room there is in the frame for fatter tyres. A 23mm wide racing tyre inflated to 120psi is super-efficient but gives a milktooth-rattling ride in a child seat. A wider, lower-pressure tyre will absorb bumps and vibrations much better.

Whatever the tyres' width, both will need to be covered with full mudguards if you're going to cycle on wet roads. Otherwise you'll spray dirty water all over your passenger. To fit mudguards, it's easiest if the frame comes with the relevant eyelets.

Here's a breakdown of some of the more suitable bike types. It's not an exhaustive list: quite a few niche bikes haven't made the cut. At least one good example of each bike type is listed. There are, of course, lots more.

MOUNTAIN BIKES

Mountain bikes are designed for riding off-road on rough tracks. There are lots of sub-genres. But for family cycling there are just two to consider: the cross-country hardtail and the urban mountain bike.

An entry-level cross-country (or XC) hardtail will have a relatively lightweight aluminium frame and a functional suspension fork. Bike control is critical on the trickier surfaces off-road, so the handlebar will be wide. Gears (21, 24 or 27) go low enough to scale any hill, and brakes (V-brake, cable disc or hydraulic disc) pack lots of power to stop you coming down. These are all plus-points for child-carrying. Tyres are wide and knobbly for better grip off-road; you're better off switching them for slick (but still fat) road tyres if that's where you'll

spend your time. Look carefully for frame-eyelets, too – some have them, some don't. Expect to pay from £250.

Trek Bike's Trek 4500 (£400, www.trekbike.co.uk) is a good entry-level XC hardtail. Compared to its peers, it keeps things simple by omitting cable disc brakes (although it comes with disc-ready hubs, so you can fit them later) and instead gets a better 27-speed drivetrain and a better suspension fork. There are mounts for a rear carrier rack and rear mudguard; fitting a front guard, however, will require some ingenuity.

The real strength of a bike like this is that you can use it for family cycling and for proper mountain biking by yourself. Quite a lot of cross-country hardtails between £250 and £500 come with the carrier rack mounts you'll want for fitting a child seat.

For around £500, the Carrera Fury (www.halfords.com) is the best of a good bunch. At around £300, the Gary Fisher Wahoo (www.fisherbikes.com) is shrewdly spec'd.

The oddly named urban mountain bike is just a cross-country style mountain bike that's kitted out for street use. A suspension fork isn't needed on road, so that's often switched for a rigid fork. Gears tend to be slightly higher, reflecting the higher speeds you ride at on road, but the range is still good, as are the brakes. Some urban mountain bikes use internal hub gearing, which is more weatherproof and reliable but has a smaller gear range. Most urban

A hybrid: the default, non-specialised bicycle
Photo: Giant CRS 2.5, Giant UK Ltd

HYBRIDS

As the name suggests, a hybrid pick-and-mixes the features of other bikes. It's the bicycle that sits right in the middle of the Venn diagram of overlapping bike varieties – the default, non-specialised bike. There are sub-genres of hybrid: sports hybrids or fitness bikes are essentially road bikes with flat handlebars; comfort bikes are more like roadsters; trekking hybrids are more like touring bikes; and the archetypal hybrid is a town-and-trail bike that looks similar to an urban mountain bike, but usually has bigger wheels.

mountain bikes do have frame eyelets for a rack and mudguards. With their mountain bike sturdiness and road-ready components, this makes them one of the better choices for a family bike. Expect to pay from £200.

The Ridgeback Cyclone (£280, www.ridgeback.co.uk) is a good value urban mountain bike. Fast-rolling slick tyres mean that tarmac work will be much easier, and the rigid fork is no handicap on road. It comes with frame eyelets for mudguards and a rear carrier rack. Ignore the disc brake mounts: you'll need new wheels to use them. Gearing is 24-speed rather than the 21-speed, offering a step up in quality as well as quantity.

The Revolution Courier (£249, www.edinburghbicycle.com) takes the keep-it-simple maxim even further, using a single chainring and an 8-speed drivetrain. It, too, is great value.
Child seat: seat-tube clamped, yes; rack fixing, maybe
Child trailer: yes
Trailer cycle: seat-post fixing, yes; rack fixing, maybe

Don't worry about the taxonomy, or whether the bike has 26-inch (mountain bike size) or '700C' (road bike size) wheels. All hybrids are viable as family bikes except perhaps the sports hybrid, which has the same pros and cons as a road bike. An entry-level hybrid has an aluminium frame, a cheap suspension fork, and fairly wide (37mm or so) lightly-treaded street tyres. Gearing is the same as that on a comparably priced urban mountain bike.

Common features include an adjustable-angle stem, which lets you move the bars closer to your body for a more upright riding position, and a cheap suspension seat-post to take the sting from bumps. Some come with accessories like mudguards and racks, and almost all can be fitted with them. As hybrids are a kind of jack-of-all-trades bike bought primarily by beginners in Britain, price and performance tend to be modest. Expect to pay from £180.

Giant's CRS 2.5 model (£299, www.giant-bicycle.com) has the features a good all-round hybrid needs: it's fairly light, in part thanks to its rigid fork, and it comes with wide enough (35mm) tyres, decent V-brakes and a 24-speed drivetrain.

There are no mudguards or carrier racks as standard, but it can be fitted with them front and rear (or see the CRS City, for £100 more). It would do fine as a general purpose commuter/leisure bike, for use on roads, cycle-ways and gentle off-road tracks.

Child seat: yes
Child trailer: yes
Trailer cycle: yes

ROADSTERS
The default transport bike in Britain up to and including the 1950s, the roadster is now a rarity. We tend to think of this sit-up-and-beg hub-geared machine as a Dutch roadster, because it's so popular there.

Roadsters are meant to be ridden fairly short distances in normal clothes. To this end they have wide saddles, an upright riding position with back-swept handlebars, and a chaincase and mudguards to keep the grime off. Many come with additional features such as a skirt guard, a kickstand, a rear carrier rack, dynamo lighting, even an integral wheel-lock.

All these useful extras add weight so roadsters are quite heavy. Aluminium

ones are seldom light, while the more traditional steel ones can weigh in at over 40lb (18kg). Street tyres mean that they still ride okay on road or well-surfaced cycle paths, however, and their get-on-and-go simplicity makes them the short-distance utility bike par excellence.

They're not so good in hilly areas. While some come with wider-range

> "Touring bikes are designed to carry a load and rider comfortably and efficiently as far they want to go"

hub gears, many have 3-speed hubs and some are single-speeds. Add high weight and hill climbing is hard, so these are best suited to flatter areas. Expect to pay from £300.

The Gazelle Esprit 3-speed (approx £440, www.gazelle.nl) is a Dutch roadster that you can buy in the UK. Available in men's and women's versions it's equipped with all the features above, and accordingly weighs about 19kg. Totally non-sporty but totally practical, it could change the way you think about city cycling – if you don't live on a hill. Traditional British roadsters are available from Pashley (www.pashley.co.uk) – complete with wicker baskets.

Child seat: yes, in flatter areas
Child trailer: yes, in flatter areas
Trailer cycle: yes, in flatter areas

TOURING BIKES

Touring bikes are designed to carry a load and rider comfortably and efficiently as far as they want to go. British touring bikes have drop handlebars, which makes them look a little like racing bikes. Touring bikes are sturdier than road bikes, with fatter tyres – often 32mm – on their 700C wheels. The gearing is from mountain bike groupsets, operated either by road bike or bar-end gear levers. The brakes are usually cantilevers, as V-brakes don't work effectively with ordinary drop-bar brake levers.

All touring bikes have provision for fitting mudguards, a rear carrier rack, and often a front rack; many are sold with them. Some touring bikes – branded 'expedition bikes' – use 26-inch wheels and more closely resemble mountain bikes than road bikes

Touring bikes are a bit longer than road bikes, which means that heels won't bash rear panniers when pedalling and toes won't overlap the front mudguard when turning. The longer wheelbase, combined with slacker frame angles, gives touring bikes steadier steering than road bikes. As with hybrids, touring bikes are capable of being ridden on towpaths, gravel tracks and the like.

Touring bikes make great family bikes, assuming you can ride confidently with a drop handlebar (possibly taking one hand off it to change gear) when you've got a child behind you. If not, the flat or butterfly bar of the trekking hybrid is the solution. Expect to pay from £400.

Touring bikes are relatively rare; many manufacturers offer just one, or even none at all. British company Dawes (www.dawescycles.com) has a whole range. The Horizon (£450) is the entry-level model. Its aluminium frame and chrome-moly steel fork have the mudguard and rack eyelets you'd expect, and it comes with them fitted. Gearing is 24-speed, mixing road levers with off-road derailleurs. The wheels are fitted with good quality 32mm touring tyres that will handle easy off-road tracks as well as tarmac. Further up the price range, Thorn Cycles (www.thorncycles.co.uk) have a good choice of tourers, especially ones with 26-inch wheels.

Child seat: yes
Child trailer: yes
Trailer cycle: yes

ROAD BIKES

The greyhounds of the cycling world, road bikes – which might better be called road racing bikes – are all about speed. Tyres are narrow and high pressure, gears are high, steering is sharp, and the narrow saddle and aerodynamic riding position are only really comfortable when wearing cycling clothes.

Road bikes are very light, thanks to a complete absence of any accessories (or even the scope to fit them) and frames constructed from expensive steel, aluminium and/or carbon fibre. Although not as fragile as they may

BATTERY FREE BIKE LIGHTS

Studies have shown that the use of bicycle safety lights reduces the number of **accidents by 40%.**

No Friction
No Batteries
Always light on
when riding the traffic

Reelights are **highly visible in traffic** whether it is day or night, summer or winter.

look, road bikes are meant for use on tarmac roads only.

For fitness or for riding fast, road bikes are unbeatable. They're better for riding by yourself than for family cycling, however. If you do want a road bike rather than hybrid or tourer for taking the kids along, look for: a triple chainset; long-reach dual-pivot sidepull brakes; the facility to fit 25 or 28mm tyres and mudguards. Expect to pay from £350.

The Specialized Allez 27 (£550, www.specialized.com) is a great entry-level racing or fitness bike. Its lightweight aluminium frame is the equal of anything in its price range, while fork and seat-post are carbon fibre. The triple chainset gives 27 gears rather than 18, which helps with hill climbing, even though they don't go as low as that of a touring or mountain bike. Clearances are too tight over even 23mm tyres for mudguards. Strong riders could use this for child trailer towing on a dry day, but really it's a bike for riding solo.

Child seat: not ideal
Child trailer: if you're strong enough!
Trailer cycle: not ideal

FOLDING BIKES

Folding bikes have one or more hinges so that the bike can folded in half – or more – to reduce its size. Most also use small wheels (16 or 20in) to make the final package as small as it can be. While the performance is seldom as good as a conventional bike when you're riding it, a folder is much easier

to cart around when you're not. You can put several in the back of car, or carry one onto a train just as you would a suitcase. Many will go on buses or coaches too, though they may need to be bagged.

The best folding bikes, such as the British-made Brompton, are marvels of metallurgical origami. They're also the easiest, and sometimes only, way

"A recumbent is more of a format than a bike type. The majority are effectively either touring or racing bikes"

for a family with more than a couple of bikes to move about the country using any transport other than the car.

Folding bikes have some limitations when it comes to family cycling. Handling tends to be a bit skittish anyway, and that's exacerbated by a child seat or trailer cycle – which will need to be seat post mounted, due to the low height of a small-wheeled folder's rack and the bike's lack of heel clearance. Brakes may not be as powerful due to convoluted cable runs, and gears often have a narrower range. Expect to pay from £300.

The classic British folding bike, which you'll see at railway stations everywhere, is the Brompton (from a little over £500, www.brompton.co.uk). It rides reasonably well for a small-wheeled bike and it folds superbly.

Like most folders, it's designed only for roads and well-surfaced tracks. If you take the train to work, a Brompton is a godsend. If you don't mind a more bulky fold, a better family-cycling option would be a bigger wheeled bike such as the Dahon Cadenza (£600, www.dahon.com). It's an urban mountain bike that folds in half and will accept a conventional rear carrier rack.

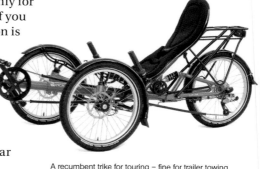

A recumbent trike for touring – fine for trailer towing
Photo: Scorpion FX, from hpvelotechnik.com

Child seat: usually not
Cycle trailer: yes (best in flatter areas)
Trailer cycle: usually not

RECUMBENTS

A recumbent bike reclines the cyclist in a kind of 'bucket seat' with the pedals out in front rather than below you. Claimed advantages include better comfort and aerodynamics. Handlebars are either above the thighs/knees, steering the front wheel directly, or under the seat, usually steering via a rod-linkage.

Bicycle recumbents typically use a small (16 or 20in) front wheel, so that it doesn't overlap the feet or push the front of the bike too high in the air; the rear wheel may be the same size or, more usually, is larger. Tricycle recumbents usually have two wheels at the front, with the rear wheel either the same size or larger.

A recumbent is more of a format than a bike type as such. The majority are effectively either touring bikes or racing bikes. Most recumbents will tow child trailers, and those that will accept a standard rear carrier rack can accommodate rack-mounting child seats or trailer cycles. They don't have a seat post, so you can't fit anything there. The main disadvantage of recumbents is cost: small-scale manufacture means high prices. They're also not so good in traffic, because slow speed stability isn't as good (at least with two-wheelers) and because your field of vision is reduced: you can't see over cars. Car drivers can usually see you just fine. Expect to pay from £1,000.

The German HP Velotechnik Street Machine (costing from £1350, www.hpvelotechnik.com) is a full-suspension touring recumbent that will tow a child trailer. It's a classic of its type, and a very comfortable way to clock up long road miles.

Child seat: sometimes, but only if rack-mounted
Child trailer: yes
Trailer cycle: sometimes, but only if rack-mounted

Babies and toddlers

UNTIL AROUND THE AGE OF FOUR, small children are non-pedalling passengers. Fortunately they're fairly portable, and at this age they're quite happy to go wherever you want to take them. The smaller they are when you start taking them cycling, the more that being out on a bike will seem like a normal, everyday activity.

A large part of cycling with small children is about having the right attitude. If you're already a cycling enthusiast, that means having a re-think about the way that you ride. Like any family trip out, a bike ride has to be geared around what the children will enjoy.

To cycle at all as a family you need the right equipment. One or more of the bikes needs adapting to carry a passenger. A child seat is the traditional answer – and at £50-£100 it's also the cheapest. Some sit the child in front of the adult, but most sit the child behind the saddle. In better weather, or when you're out for a day ride with a toddler, a child seat is a good choice. However, it does compromise the handling of the bike and leaves your passenger exposed to the elements.

A child trailer is a two-wheeled buggy that fixes to the adult's bike with an articulating towbar. One or two children sit inside on stroller-style hammock seats. Prices are higher than for child seats, ranging from £80 to over £600. They're worth the extra, and not only because the average family has two children rather than one. A trailer gives extra room for toys, nappies, spare clothes, even groceries, and its cover provides protection from the weather and insects. Bike handling isn't affected much. And despite the child sitting lower down, safety is actually better than with a child seat.

Most expensive of all are special cycles specifically designed to carry children. Many have a tricycle layout with two front wheels and a covered box between them. You'll have to buy such cycles from a specialist in the UK.

However you choose to cycle, it can feel like an expedition just getting yourself, your kids, and assorted paraphernalia out of the front door. Stick with it – it gets easier! One big bonus from making the effort is that the gentle motion from cycling makes smaller children fall asleep, in the same way as placing them in a car seat or pushchair.

Child seats

MOST CHILD SEATS are suitable for children between the ages of about nine months and four years. The lower limit is dependent on the ability of your child to sit up unsupported – that is, on the floor rather than propped up with cushions. Some seats recline and children as young as six months – those who can sit up when propped up – can go in those. A reclining seat is better anyway because it allows junior to drift off to sleep without slumping sideways or forwards.

The upper limit is restricted by weight rather than age. Seats are typically rated for passengers weighing up to around 20kg (44lb). Even if a seat seems sturdy enough to take a heavier child than that, it's a bad idea to exceed its weight limit. It's not so much that the seat will break – although it might – rather that the handling of the bike gets progressively worse with a heavier passenger, particularly with a rear-fitting seat.

FRONT-FITTING SEATS

Front seats usually attach to the top tube, a bar fixed above it, or a bracket on the head tube. Some are moulded plastic seats, like smaller versions of rear seats, while others – aimed at older children who can hold on themselves – are just little saddles and footrests bolted to the bike.

Both types of front seat have the advantage that your child can see more and can talk to you more easily. You end up pedalling awkwardly – knees out, like John Wayne on a bike – but balance is actually better, particularly over bumps. Your child is slightly more exposed to wind chill, though. More seriously, in the event of a fall your child can end up acting as your airbag.

If you do want a front-fitting seat, Dutch company Bobike make ones suitable for 1-2 year olds that can be fitted with a windscreen (Front Mini, £90 including windscreen, www.amba-marketing.com). This greatly helps to protect against wind chill and rain. For children aged up to four or so, the Weeride Kangaroo (£60, formerly known as the Centric Safe Haven) is a better choice because it's designed for a heavier passenger. See www.weeride.co.uk.

Those little saddles that bolt to the top tube aren't recommended for anything other than short journeys. A tired child could slip sideways or let a foot dangle into the front wheel, with predictably dangerous results.

It's possible to use front and rear seats on the same bike, but unless you live somewhere flat, doing so makes the bike very cumbersome. A child trailer is a superior solution for two children. If you need just the one seat, then, despite its handling quirks, the pedalling and safety advantages of a rear seat make it the better option.

Photo: Cycling Images

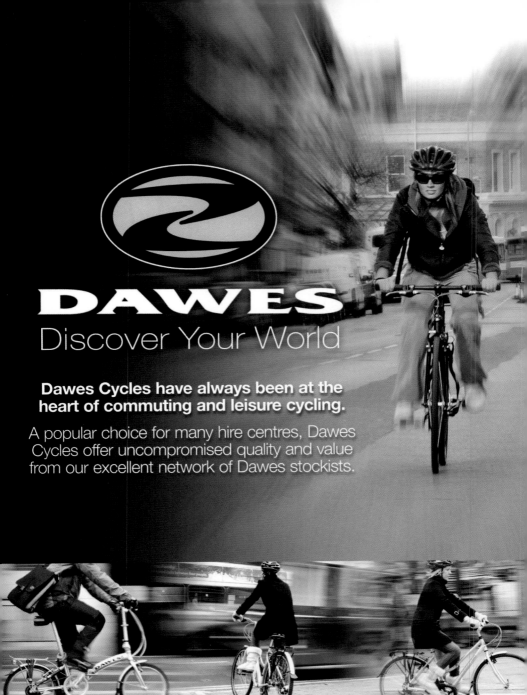

DAWES
Discover Your World

Dawes Cycles have always been at the heart of commuting and leisure cycling.

A popular choice for many hire centres, Dawes Cycles offer uncompromised quality and value from our excellent network of Dawes stockists.

Dawes Cycles Ltd. 35 Tameside Drive Castle Bromwich Birmingham B35 7AG
Tel: 0121 7488050 **www.dawescycles.com**

The market-leading Copilot Limo is a rear-fitting child seat with the ability to recline, which gives a better ride for a sleeping child. It also features a pivoting grab bar as well as a safety harness, and can even be used as a baby chair once detached from the bike

REAR-FITTING SEATS

Rear seats come in three basic designs: cantilevered from the seat tube; fixed to a rear carrier rack; and fixed directly to the seat tube and seat stays. Those that bolt to the frame – or to a rack that's bolted to the frame – are more stable and sturdy but cannot be fitted to bikes with rear suspension.

Cantilevered seats use a big plastic bracket with two holes in it bolted to the seat tube. Into this slots a two-pronged rack that supports the seat. There's some give in the rack, which offers a degree of springy suspension. This may not flex enough under smaller children, leaving them tipped slightly forwards. Larger children

and/or long-term use may flex it too far, bending it down towards the rear tyre or mudguard. Typically the more you pay, the sturdier the seat will be. The Hamax Sleepy (£60, www.fisheroutdoor.co.uk) is one of the better examples. It has a decent attachment bracket and the seat can be reclined.

Seats that fix to a rear carrier rack slide and lock onto the rack's top, with a safety strap around the seat-post or seat-tube for added security. With the seat off, the rack can be used to carry panniers. The £100 Copilot Limo (www.ultimatepursuits.co.uk) is the best of these designs and has for some years set the standard in child seats.

The Limo reclines to give a better ride to a sleeping child. Its harness is supplemented by a pivoting grab-bar, like the safety bar on a roller-coaster carriage. What's more, you can rotate this bar over the back of the seat to turn it into a baby chair when it's off the bike – so you don't need to wake your sleeping tot at journey's end. The cheaper Copilot Taxi (£80, also at www.ultimatepursuits.co.uk) is just as sturdy but doesn't recline or convert to a baby chair.

Seats that fix directly to the seat stays and seat tube have long legs that bolt to the seat stays, often using a quick-release, plus a bracket that fits on the seat tube to prevent fore and aft movement. The Bobike Maxi (£75, www.amba-marketing.com) is a good one. It's well made, with a maximum load of 25kg. That should be enough for a six-year-old child, assuming you can still balance the bike properly.

Most seats fit best on medium or larger sized bikes with a conventional top tube. Small frames and those with a dropped top tube can cause fitting difficulties for any seat that uses a seat tube bracket. Open frames – that is, frames without a top tube – can flex and shimmy alarmingly when you're cycling with a heavier child on a rear seat, because the structure isn't stiff enough. Look for fatter frame tubes and/or reinforcing tubes if you want to fit this kind of bike with a child seat.

Small-wheeled folding bikes tend to handle poorly when fitted with a child seat, even where this is possible (usually by fitting a cantilevered seat). Recumbent cycles don't have the seat tube that some seats require, but any bike or trike that can be fitted with a conventional rear carrier rack can take rack-fitting seats. Tandems (see Chapter 3) can be fitted with rear child seats and are much less affected by handling issues. Upright tricycles with two wheels at the back can take two child seats between the wheels, facing forwards or back.

> "A reclining seat is better because it allows junior to drift off to sleep without slumping sideways or forwards"

SAFETY

Feet in spokes account for half of all child hospital admissions that involve child seats. Footrests are not enough; feet may slip off or your child may simply forget and let legs dangle. It's essential that any seat has secure foot straps, ideally in wraparound foot wells. Be aware of what else might reach the spokes – items such as scarfs, mittens on strings, and long laces – and make sure they can't. The skirt guard that's fitted to Dutch roadsters is a useful extra barrier.

Little fingers can also get caught, usually in an adult's sprung saddle rather than the spokes. If your saddle has springs, either swap it for one that doesn't or make or buy a finger guard. Bobike's Saddle Spring Protector is what you need if you don't fancy doing some DIY using a strip of stiff plastic and some zip ties.

To keep your child secure, most seats use a three-point harness, with straps going over the shoulders and securing between the legs. A better set-up is to have a waist belt or bar as well, as toddlers can sometimes slip out of shoulder straps when asleep. Seats that tilt back alleviate this problem, because your child won't be slumping into the straps.

Child seats aren't as conspicuous as child trailers or trailer cycles when you're on the road, and some drivers won't give you such a wide berth. If that's a problem where you ride, consider a bright 'baby on board' sticker or a flashing LED light fixed to the child seat.

COMFORT

Seats should offer full back and head support. Even then, a sleeping child's neck won't be well supported so it's best if the seat also reclines. If it does, you can also use an inflatable, horseshoe-shaped neck pillow (from baby shops, and intended for use in car seats) for even better support.

Some kind of seat padding is essential, and it should be readily removable so you can wash it. Recently potty-trained kids will wet themselves at some point, usually when you forget to bring spare pants and trousers! For greater comfort, use fatter tyres on

Protect children from the elements in summer as well as winter
Photo: istock

your bike and run them at a slightly lower pressure; the bigger air pocket in the tyres will 'eat' bumps and absorb vibration better.

Off-road, stick to smooth tracks to prevent bouncing your child around. Save mountain biking proper until your child is old enough for his or her own bike, or at least the back of a tandem. A fall off-road at an early age could deter your child from cycling even if it doesn't result in serious injury, while shaken baby syndrome is a risk for infants forced to endure choppy singletrack. A youngster in a child seat can't move around to absorb impacts like you and so will feel every jolt. It's common sense, really.

Weather protection is also essential. Children on child seats get cold very easily as they're not generating heat like the person doing the cycling. Put at least one extra layer on your child than on you – fleece-lined all-in-one outdoor romper suits are good, as are salopettes in winter.

When cycling in Britain you'll also need rain protection. Soggy kids can get chilled quickly. You could adapt a buggy rain cover or a canoe spray deck, or you can buy a dedicated child seat cape from Edinburgh Bicycle Co-op (£15, www.edinburghbicycle.com). This will help keep the wind off as well as the rain.

In summer, children in seats burn easily – especially on the back of the neck if they slump forward. Use plenty of high factor barrier cream. On sunnier days you might even want to fit a cap under their helmet – a traditional cotton cycling cap for adults fits surprisingly well.

Flies and wasps can freak out small children, who often attract them by being sticky. Take wet wipes on any ride that will involve eating or use some kind of repellent.

USEFUL EXTRAS

To use a child seat on more than one bike – on mum's as well as dad's, for example – buy an extra rack or bracket for the seat when you purchase it. While seats are usually quick-release, racks and brackets stay fixed to the bike because they take minutes rather than seconds to remove.

It can be tricky getting a child into and out of a child seat if you're on your own, even with a wall to lean the bike against. Toddlers are heavy and it only takes a foot snagged in a seat strap when you're lifting your child to send the bike crashing to the ground. The Esge Twin Leg Kickstand (£17, www.chickencycles.co.uk) looks like a motorcycle propstand and is one of the few kickstands strong enough to hold bike and child upright while you sort out buckles and straps. That said, you should never leave a child in a seat unattended. It doesn't take much to tip over a top-heavy bicycle.

If you find it hard to balance when looking round with your passenger

A twin-leg kickstand holds the bike while you get junior aboard
Photo: Cycling Images

on board, then it's a good idea to fit a handlebar mirror such as the Busch und Müller CycleStar (£13-£15, www.amba-marketing.com). Not only will you be able to monitor traffic behind you, you'll also be able to see if your child has fallen asleep.

"Don't be tempted to stand up on the pedals to power uphill. The bike handles better with your weight on the saddle"

Some child seats come with an integral reflector on the back, but few have mounting points for lights, which you must use if you're riding after dusk. As a seat post light will be obscured by the seat, your best bet is to mount a light on the back of the carrier rack.

If you're planning to walk with your child at the end of your ride, the Steco Buggy Mee Deluxe is a great help (it's Dutch but can be ordered direct for 25 Euros from www.babycare.nl). It's an adapter for the rear rack that enables it to carry a folded-up pushchair. It fits to one side of the bike and projects backwards, and so won't interfere with your rear-fitting child seat.

RIDING WITH A CHILD SEAT

Even if you're used to riding with rear panniers, a child seat takes some getting used to. Panniers put the weight around or between the axles. Child seats put the weight above and

Cantilevered seats fit best on bikes with a standard top tube
Photo: Dan Joyce

– more significantly – behind the rear axle, which destabilises the bike. Get a plumb line to check where the base of the seat is relative to the rear axle. The shorter the distance it is behind the axle, the better the handling will be. If it's level or in front, so much the better. There's no hard and fast maximum distance, but keeping it under 10cm is a reasonable rule of thumb.

Before you ride with your child on the seat try loading it up with a heavy weight, such as a 7-10kg sack of potatoes, and take it for a ride. That will give you a clear idea of how different the bike will feel with a passenger on the seat. At first, you will wobble, particularly at slow speeds.

2.2 Child seats

An extra bracket or rack for your child seat means that you can swap it from bike to bike between or even during rides
Photo: Cycling Images.

Don't be tempted to stand up on the pedals to power uphill. The bike will handle better with your weight on the saddle, so change down the gears and spin instead. If that fails, get off. It's easier than you might think to fall when you're going up a steep hill. (I did it twice in eight years of child seat use. The wraparound seat prevented any injury to my passenger both times, but it was still a nasty shock – and I took some nasty gouges.)

You can stabilise the unbalancing effect of a rear seat to some degree by using low-rider panniers on the front of the bike and filling them with the picnic, toddler paraphernalia or shopping. The extra weight around the front wheel will steady the steering and keep the tyre on the tarmac – especially uphill, where the lightly-loaded front end can otherwise become skittish.

Front seats don't have such a dramatic effect on handling, but it's still worth taking the aforementioned spin with the spuds so that you get a feel for riding the loaded bike.

Unless you have a step-through frame, you will need to practice getting on and off the bike with the child seat in place. If you swing your leg over the saddle like you're used to doing, you'll risk kicking your passenger in the head. Instead you need to step over the top tube.

**Designed and manufactured in Germany, with children in mind
Environmentally friendly materials**

Distributed by Amba Marketing 01392 829903
See www.pukydirect.com for details and stockists.

**Top quality range of child trailers. Suitable for babies.
Multi functional as a trailer, buggy or stroller.**

Distributed by Amba Marketing 01392 829903
www.amba-marketing.com Ring for further details and stockists.

Child trailers

A CHILD TRAILER is the single most useful accessory for family cycling. It's the pedaller's equivalent to the pram or pushchair. Most trailers seat two children, with a maximum recommended load of 45kg (100lb). A few seat just one child.

The recommended age range is similar to a child-seat: nine months (the sitting up stage) to about five years. In fact, it can be wider than this. Some trailers, notably by Chariot (www.amba-marketing.com) and Winther (www.winther-bikes.com) have an optional baby supporter that can be fitted to a seat to allow a child as young as three months to sit in a kind of sling alongside a sibling.

Alternatively, you can secure an infant's car seat into a cycle trailer using luggage straps. You'll only get one child in the trailer this way, and it's something that North American trailer manufacturers sternly advise against – no doubt to prevent possible legal action. It does work, however, so long as you ride responsibly and stick to smooth roads. You can use a baby neck cushion to improve comfort. My own boys travelled this way from just a few weeks old.

TRAILER DESIGNS

The typical child trailer is a two-seater with a frame made from aluminium tubing and covered with polyester fabric. The seats hang down hammock-style from one of the cross tubes and there are plastic windows at the sides; the front usually rolls up in better weather so that a breeze can enter via an insect-screen. Wheels are either 16 or 20-inches with conventional pneumatic tyres. Total weight is around 10 or 11kg unloaded.

Solid-bottomed trailers are a bit heavier, at around 13-14kg. The plastic base won't wear through at the foot-well like even reinforced polyester can. It's better in wet weather, especially if the plastic moulding extends over the wheels to form wheel arches as these will act as mudguards. However, a solid-bottomed trailer is a lot noisier, since the plastic base is liable to reverberate like a drum.

"Trailers are more comfortable than child seats, as the children sit in suspended, hammock-style seats"

Often the wheels and towbar of either type of trailer are quick release, and the sides will fold down flat. A couple of minutes' work gives you a package small enough for the boot of a car, or even to take on a train. Folding also helps where space is at a premium and the trailer has to be stored in the house or flat, or where it has to pass through a door or gate that's narrower

A trailer allows children to bring along favourite books or toys, and to keep each other company. A seat harness keeps them secure
Photos: Carlton Reid

than it is. Plenty are. While a bike will go through any door, trailers usually measure 75-80cm across at their widest point.

Measure any space the trailer will need to pass through and check it against the trailer's specification before you buy. One trailer might be a few centimetres narrower than another, which could be just enough of a difference for it not to need folding. That won't just save you several minutes when you go out, it will also mean that you can leave a sleeping child in the trailer when you get home.

Trailers that accommodate one child are a bit narrower and lighter, although only by around 10cm and a kilogramme. The wheels have to be a reasonable width apart or the trailer wouldn't be stable.

More expensive trailers have optional kits that convert them to strollers or push chairs, comprising a push bar at the back and an extra wheel or two at the front. When converted like they work like normal strollers, albeit bulky ones. Some trailers even have ski conversion kits!

GETTING HITCHED

Trailers have less effect on the handling of the towing bike if they attach low down by the rear axle rather than up high on the seatpost, so that's what virtually all current trailers do.

Since the towbar pivots right by the hitch, having the hitch further back also limits the extent to which the trailer cuts corners as it follows the towing bike.

Sometimes the hitch is permanently attached to the end of the towing arm and clamps around the left-hand chain stay and/or seat stay. This allows an easy switch between any bikes with a conventional rear triangle. However, a rear disc or drum brake and some hub gear torque arms can foul this type of hitch.

Other hitches bolt semi-permanently to the towing bike's axle (get extra hitches for extra bikes), with a simple link and pin arrangement on the towing arm. Different hitches – Burley (www.fisheroutdoor.co.uk) offer three different types – allow for fitting to most common types of bike.

Whatever hitch the trailer uses, it must have a safety strap so that if the main hitch comes loose the trailer won't detach from the towing bike.

SAFETY

'Is that safe?' If you use a child trailer another parent will ask you this, or at least think it. The answer is yes. Unless you ride very rashly indeed, your child is not at risk from cycling itself while in a trailer. Unlike a child seat passenger, trailer passengers aren't in danger if the adult falls: the trailer, having two wheels, should remain upright. Even if it doesn't, the trailer has less distance to fall and the occupants are strapped in and surrounded by a rollcage.

The canopy rolls up for access. In use, the insect screen at least would be down. Photo: Andy Shrimpton

Traffic looks more dangerous because children sit low down in a trailer, just as they do in a pushchair. Yet whenever trailers have been tested they've been found to be safer than seats in a crash.

In any situation involving traffic, whether you're a pedestrian on a pavement or a passenger in a car, there's always a small degree of risk. Safety comes primarily from not being involved in a collision in the first place.

In that respect, trailers are a help rather than a hindrance. They're highly visible, not only because of their bright colours but because their novelty value makes them conspicuous. A driver will no more fail to notice a child trailer than he would fail to notice a bright yellow dustbin in the middle of the road. What's more, the width of the trailer discourages drivers from trying to squeeze past in dangerously tight situations. Those drivers who recognise a child trailer for what it is afford you even more respect – just as they would for a parent pushing a pram across a zebra crossing.

Many trailers come with bright orange safety flags. Whether these make a bright trailer much more visible is debatable, but it's unlikely they do any harm.

COMFORT

Trailers are more comfortable than child seats. As the seats are suspended hammock-style there's a degree of shock absorbency over bumps and ruts. Some trailers also have suspension systems similar to those used on mountain bikes for even better bump isolation.

Those that don't still have the pneumatic suspension of the tyres. Don't diminish that by pumping the trailer tyres as hard as your bike tyres. With a lighter load than your bike's – much lighter with only one child aboard – you can afford to run trailer tyres at a lower pressure. It will increase drag slightly but greatly improve comfort for your passenger. Try running the trailer tyres at the minimum pressure recommended on the tyre sidewall.

Weatherproofing is obviously better

in a trailer too. You still need to wrap your child up warm as there's no insulation to speak of, but the canopy keeps the wind off. It will also keep most of the rain out. In really wet weather, water can sometimes get in and pool in the footwell – so don't forget the wellies if you're setting off into a downpour! The canopy keeps overhead sun off, too, and the insect mesh stops flies and wasps annoying jammy-faced passengers.

Children are often happier in a trailer because a favourite toy can come along for the ride, without the risk that Flopsy will be dropped into the road and lost. When two children travel together, they can keep each other company – which is usually all to the good but occasionally means arguing and pinching.

USEFUL FEATURES

All trailers, even soft-bottomed ones, can carry things like groceries around, too. You can usually get a fair load in the trailer even with one or two children, so long as you pack only light things next to passengers. (Be warned that toddlers will start to chew on the shopping if anything is within reach!)

Where there's a separate storage area, such as behind the seats, there's a bit more freedom to fill it with shopping. Solid bottom trailers, on the other hand, can carry a broader range of cargo loads in lieu of children, because you won't tear the base. Really heavy loads could crack the base, however, so keep to the recommended load limit even if you're on the way home from a hardware store.

Some trailers have internal side-pockets next to the seats. These are handy for teddies and snacks, as a strapped-in child won't be able to reach items that fall into the footwell.

On the outside, reflective Scotchlite

> "Trailers can cost anywhere from £80 to over £600, with most of the better quality ones starting at about £200"

strips make a trailer much more visible in the dark. For use at night, the trailer must be fitted with a red rear reflector and a red rear light, which should be fitted to the off-side at the back. You can usually clip a small LED light on somewhere, although dedicated mounting points make this easier.

To help keep the sun off, some trailers have tinted side windows. If yours has clear windows, you may need to rig up some kind of sun screen inside the trailer on a really hot day. A spare jumper or jacket hanging down from the cross-struts should do it, or you can use one of those screens that go on car side windows.

The towing bike needs a full-length rear mudguard, ideally with a mudflap, if you plan to use the trailer on wet roads. Otherwise dirty water will be sprayed over and possibly into the front of the trailer. You will need to clean it with soapy water from time to time just to deal with the water thrown up by the trailer's own wheels.

RIDING WITH A CHILD TRAILER

Child trailers are very stable, with a low centre of gravity, so there are no bike balance issues to worry about. They do add quite a lot of drag, though, because of the extra weight, wheels, and wind resistance. You'll feel this on even the slightest hill, so the towing bike needs a low bottom gear.

Good brakes are equally important when descending but shouldn't be used suddenly because the trailer can then shunt the towing bike, which is obviously disconcerting. This is the reason trailers are limited to a load of around 45kg.

The width of the trailer takes some getting used to. Eventually your trailer antenna will develop to the point where you'll know at a glance if you can fit between those cycleway bollards. Until then take it easy, and be prepared to detach the trailer and wheel it around or lift it over barriers.

Even with a pivot point close to the towing bike's rear axle trailers still cut in whenever you corner, a bit like an articulated lorry. To prevent it from clipping kerbs, you'll need to take a slightly wider line when you're turning. If you forget this when you're going fast and the inside wheel hits the kerb, it's possible to flip the trailer. It's something I've only ever done and seen done with an empty trailer, which flips much more easily than an

Low gears and good brakes make trailer towing much easier. In summer, mudguards aren't always essential
Photo: Andy Shrimpton

occupied one, but even that should serve as a warning against riding ridiculously fast with children aboard.

WHICH TRAILER?

Child trailers cost anywhere from £80 to over £600, with most better quality ones starting at about £200. The Burley Bee (£250, www.fisheroutdoor.co.uk) is a good, basic, two-seater trailer. It folds to 89 x 76 x 31cm and weighs less than 10kg. Capacity is the usual 45kg.

If that seems a little too expensive, then the two-seater Revolution Roller (www.edinburghbicycle.com) is half the price at £119. It's made from tubular steel instead of aluminium so it's heavier (14.5kg) but it still folds flat

and has useful features like internal pockets and a roll-up raincover.

Paying more gets you a more comfortable, more fully-featured trailer that handles slightly better. Good brand names in trailers are: Burley (who have several models other than the aforementioned Bee), Winther (www.winther-bikes.com) Chariot and Croozer (the latter two from www.amba-marketing.com).

The Chariot Carriers CX 2 (£640) is a Rolls-Royce among trailers, with smooth suspension, a fast fold, and lots of nice touches. It converts easily to a stroller, and as such can be equipped with a sling to fit a child as young as one month old.

Special bikes

IF YOU PLAN to be cycling with children on a regular, perhaps daily, basis it can be worth making a bigger investment in the form of a dedicated child-carrying cycle. You don't see these often on the streets of Britain. Across the North Sea in Denmark and Holland, where any that do exist in the UK are imported from, they're all over the place.

Prices typically range from about £1,000 to £2,000 or more. If that sounds a lot, consider that over the course of four or five pre-school years it amounts to pennies per trip. Carrier cycles don't become redundant when children graduate to their own bikes either, since they're equally effective at carrying other loads once any seating has been removed.

The reverse is true as well. Many load carrying cycles will also carry children. Some have off-the-peg child carrying adaptations available from the manufacturer, while others will need you to fix child car seats or some such in place.

This is perfectly legal and, with a bit of common sense, quite safe. Carrier bikes only travel at the kind of pace you could run. It's not like making a DIY car or motorbike seat. If you do choose to go down this route, then do remember that seatbelts of some kind are essential for younger children and little fingers must not be able to reach the wheels.

TWO-WHEELERS

Bicycle child carriers are easier to live with than tricycles. They're not as wide, so gates, cycle track barriers and so forth are less of a problem. They're also easier to ride, in that you don't have to 'unlearn' your cycling skills to steer them as you do with a trike.

A load platform or box sits low down either in front of or behind the rider, and as so has minimal effect on balance, even with a two children aboard. For parking, most have a two-legged stand under the load platform. It's a little easier to ride when the load is behind. However, you can keep an eye on your passengers if the load box is in front.

The Dutch Bakfiets CargoBike has a front box with a bench in there for two children, and an optional rain cover. Prices start at £1,150. It's available from a couple of suppliers in the UK (www.velorution.biz and also www.thisisloadsbetter.com).

A slightly cheaper implementation of the same idea is the Gazelle Cabby (£1,000, www.cycle-heaven.co.uk). There's also the British-made Burrows 8Freight, which has the cargo area behind the rider. Prices start at £1,250 (www.bikefix.co.uk). It's a cargo bike, pure and simple, so it's necessary to sort your own child seating.

An interesting new bike is the Yuba Mundo, which looks like a conventional bicycle with a stretched rear end and an integral rack. It's designed as a load- and people-carrying transport bike for Africa, although it's just as useful for the same jobs in the UK. With footrests, two school age children could sit pillion-style on the back. Or you could fit two frame-fitting child seats there. What's more, it only costs around £400 (www.thisisloadsbetter.com).

For slightly less outlay, you can convert a conventional bicycle into a similar stretched load carrier using an Xtracycle FreeRadical (£295, same source). This bolts on a kind of extra rear triangle and carrier support to the back end of a bike.

THREE-WHEELERS
Tricycles add bulk and cost but also capacity: the biggest will carry up to a quarter of a tonne – if you can pedal it! Riding a trike takes some acclimatisation. The first few times

you get on one you may find that you steer it into the kerb. On a bicycle, some of the steering comes from balancing and leaning. On a trike it doesn't, and the steering is more like being in a car than on a bike. In theory that's straightforward, but a bicycle saddle and handlebars may persuade your brain that it's controlling a two-wheeler. Stick with it: it's not hard to ride a trike, just different.

The Danish Christiania trike, which has a front box between its two wheels, will carry up to four children if fitted with two benches. Like the Bakfiets CargoBike, there's a big rain canopy available for it. Prices start at £1,100, from Velorution (www.velorution.biz). There are even bigger Dutch carrier trikes like this – which will carry up to eight children – but you'll need to go all the way to Amsterdam to get one, or else arrange the shipping yourself. See www.workbikes.com for more.

There is also a huge British trike available: the Cycles Maximus (www.cyclesmaximus.com). In its pedicab-rickshaw format, which you may recognise from the streets of London, it will carry three adults plus rider, while its soft-top cargo layout could, with the addition of benches, probably carry six children. However, this configuration does cost £3,300.

The Danish Christiania trike can be fitted with one or two benches to fit two or four pirates. Photo: Christiania Bikes

BY THE TIME they start school most children are capable of riding a bicycle of their own. They won't be able to ride it very far or very fast, of course, and there are some journeys, such as those involving busier roads, where you might not want them to ride solo. But that doesn't mean they have to travel as non-pedalling passengers.

The cheapest solution is a trailer cycle, which is basically half a child's bike plus a towbar to attach it to your bike. Prices start at around £100. Most suit children from age four to nine. As with child seats, the upper limit is dictated by weight: a trailer cycle passenger shouldn't exceed about half your bodyweight. A heavier trailer cycle rider gives a tail-wags-dog effect, making it harder to control the bike.

A tandem is a big step up from a trailer cycle in terms of price, with new ones costing £800 or more. Bike handling is much better, too, and the half-your-bodyweight rule for your pedalling passenger no longer applies, although it's easier if the person steering is the heavier and stronger rider.

There are two ways to get a child on a tandem. You can adapt an all-adult tandem using bolt-on 'kiddy cranks' to put a set of pedals high up on the bike's frame at the back, where a small child's legs can reach. Or you can buy a child-back tandem, which slopes steeply down from the front (adult rider) to the back (child rider). Instead of bringing the pedals up to the child, a child-back tandem moves the saddle down to where the pedals are.

Whether using a trailer cycle or a tandem, your child will be actively cycling but under your control. Only you can steer and brake. You can ride pretty much anywhere, while providing a gentle introduction to cycling skills and traffic sense by commenting on what you're doing.

If you've got two or more children, you can put one child on the back of tandem and add a child seat, child trailer or trailer cycle. Or both parents can tow trailer cycles or use tandems. You can even buy tandems with three seats, known as triplets.

If you've got a child who's too big for a child trailer or child seat but has balance problems or some other disability that would rule out a conventional trailer cycle or tandem, don't worry – there are solutions. Some involve pedalling, some don't.

Trailer cycles

A TRAILER CYCLE is essentially a child's bicycle with the front wheel, fork and headset replaced by a long towbar or boom. It fits to the back of an adult's bike to form an articulated tandem. You and your child can make trips that are faster, further and safer than you could manage on separate bikes. Your son or daughter can help out by pedalling or, when tired, can simply be towed along. Unlike most tandems, all trailer cycles have an independent freewheel.

Trailer cycles are much cheaper than tandems and take up much less space.

They're more versatile too, in that you can detach the trailer cycle and have a normal solo bike as required. The trailer cycle has been around since the 1930s, when it was invented in England by Bill Rann. Recently it's enjoyed something of a renaissance, although with a few notable exceptions the modern versions are actually worse than the Rann trailers of yesteryear.

That's because most modern trailer cycles attach to and pivot at the seatpost. A much better arrangement, used by Rann in the past and by Burley and Islabikes today, has the trailer

Rack-mounted trailer cycles such as this Islabikes Trailerbike handle much better than seatpost-mounted trailer cycles
Photo: Islabikes

cycle's vertical (pitch) and horizontal (turn) pivots directly above the towing bike's rear axle. To attach here such designs use a rear rack that's like, and often doubles as, a pannier rack.

All one-wheeled trailer cycles will cope with gentle off-road terrain and all can be taken touring. Most bikes can tow a trailer cycle. Only those that will accept a standard rear carrier rack can tow rack-mounted trailer cycles. Such bikes are a good choice in any case because they're designed be ridden with a load. Bikes that aren't, such as road bikes and most folding bikes, can handle very poorly when you add on a trailer cycle.

Good trailer cycles such as Burleys and Islabikes hold their value well, so you may struggle to find a bargain second hand. The flip side is that you should get a good price for yours when your children finally outgrow it.

TRAILER CYCLE DESIGNS

Most trailer cycles have one wheel. Some have two and look like the back end of a tricycle, while others have none. The latter type – of which the TrailGator (£70, www.trail-gator.co.uk) is the best current example – is a towbar that fixes to your child's existing bike to turn it into an ersatz trailer cycle. The attachment process locks out the steering on the child's bike and may involve removal of the front wheel. It's a versatile solution because you can convert trailer cycle to child's bike, or vice-versa, mid-ride. In practice, bike handling is much the

same as with other seatpost-mounted trailer cycles – i.e. just about adequate – although it isn't as sturdy.

Single wheel trailer cycles come in two types: seatpost or rack mounted. Most attach at the seatpost because that design is cheap and easy to make. The trailer cycle articulates on plain bearings. At best, the turn pivot is vertical and on a bracket that's behind the seatpost; at worst, the turn pivot *is* the seatpost. Since a bike's seatpost isn't vertical (it's around 72 degrees rather than 90), this leads to a peculiar handling quirk in which the trailer cycle leans out on corners.

Handling problems are compounded by the plain bearings: there's a fine line between too tight, which means the trailer won't articulate properly, and too loose, which gives slop or play at the joint, letting the trailer cycle rock from side to side. This feels like someone grabbing hold of the seatpost of your bike and trying to twist it from side to side. So you need to set up seatpost hitches with care.

The Avenir T100 tag-a-long from Raleigh (£120, www.raleigh.co.uk) is a good example of a seatpost-mounted trailer cycle, as it's one of the few that gets the turn pivot right. It also folds and has a full chain case. It's single speed, but for £20 more a geared version is available.

Rack-fixing trailer cycles are somewhat more rare. The Burley Piccolo (www.fisheroutdoor.co.uk) has been the benchmark for some years, thanks to its excellent handling. Not

only does the Piccolo have the pivots above the towing bike's rear axle, like the Rann, it improved on the design. The turn pivot is fixed to the rack, with the pitch (vertical) pivot behind it on the towing arm. This stops the trailer cycle flopping or jackknifing when it's being pushed along on foot. The Piccolo dropped out of production briefly as Burley focused on its child trailers. For 2008, it's back. The UK price hadn't been announced as the book went to press, although in previous years it was around £350.

The Islabikes Trailerbike (£200, www.islabikes.co.uk) is similar. Previously it had a rack hitch like the Rann, but now it's been improved so it's like the Burley's. Like the Piccolo, it comes with a custom carrier rack for the towing bike, which you can use for panniers too. It even comes supplied with a mudguard.

> "All one-wheeled trailer cycles will be able to cope with gentle off-road terrain and all can be taken touring"

Trailer cycles with two rear wheels – trailer tricycles, if you like – are heavier and more awkward to store than single wheelers but are much better for heavier loads. With a single-wheel trailer cycle, you're ill advised to ride with a child more than half your own weight because the twisting forces that the trailer cyclist exerts on the towing bike can upset the steering. A trailer tricycle won't tip the towing bike's balance like this because it doesn't lean; it's always upright.

If you would struggle to control a single wheeler, either because you're light or because you want to tow a heavier child, a trailer tricycle is a more stable option. The Pashley U-Plus-1 (£445, www.pashley.co.uk) can additionally be fitted with a backrest using a chest strap (£85), the better to keep a child with balance problems in the saddle. The same is true of Pashley's bigger Add-1 (also £85), which can be used by teenagers and adults. Pashley also used to make a two-wheeler for two children, the U-Plus-2. It's no longer in production, although you may be able to pick one up second hand.

UNDERSTANDING HANDLING
Even the best trailer cycle doesn't ride as surely as a good tandem. Partly it's because the bit doing the steering – your bike – has a shorter wheelbase than a tandem combined with steering geometry that's optimised for a solo bicycle. Mostly, however, it's because the bike-plus-trailer cycle articulates and you've got a weight behind you that can twist, tug and shunt the towing bike at the attachment point. So the better the attachment point is designed, the better the overall handling will be.

Rack-mounted trailer cycles handle much better than seatpost-mounted ones. Instead of pivoting on plain

3.2 Trailer cycles

Most trailer cycles pivot on the same axis as the seatpost, which isn't vertical. Cornering can be odd. Photo: Cycling Images

cycle tracks and the like. Things get erratic when the hitch has too much play or the passenger is too heavy. Just riding along on a flat road suddenly becomes a trial. This is why it's a bad idea to have a single wheel trailer cycle for two passengers. Bike handling isn't just bad, it's dangerous. You don't see many two-seaters like this around, but Adams used to make one. If you do see one second hand, avoid it. In over 15 years working as a cycle journalist it's the most dangerous thing I've ever taken out on the road.

Trailer tricycles are a different matter. Balance isn't a problem, even with two passengers or a heavier load, because the trailer part doesn't lean-steer. A seatpost hitch is fine, so long as the turn pivot is vertical rather than parallel to the seatpost. Ideally you want some kind of ball joint rather than a universal joint, so that the bicycle (towing bike) and tricycle (trailer cycle) can corner without the bicycle trying to make the tricycle lean – something it can only do with one wheel in the air!

The difference in cornering between towing bike and trailer tricycle is not a problem at modest speeds – say, 15mph and below. It is a problem if you hit a corner going faster, especially if it's off-camber. Trailer tricycle passengers must lean into the corner or the trailer cycle may roll out of the corner onto its side. Similarly, it's easy to flip an unoccupied trailer tricycle if it clips a kerb at speed. If you ride with a degree of restraint,

bearings they can take advantage of ball bearings so that they turn as sweetly as the headset on your own bike, moving freely but without play. The attachment point of a rack-mounted trailer cycle is right above the towing bike's rear axle rather than in front of it, so it tracks better after the towing bike instead of cutting corners. Effectively the attachment point is a bit lower down, too: it's connected, via the carrier rack, to the towing bike's seat stays and rear dropouts. That means the trailer cycle has less leverage to tug at the towing bike.

With a relatively light passenger, seatpost-mounted trailer cycles can nevertheless handle adequately for

everything will be fine without any motorcycle-sidecar-style leaning. You can, of course, remove any handling disparities by coupling a trailer tricycle to the back of a tricycle.

Note that a trailer tricycle may try to twist around the towbar, assuming it's fixed to a bicycle without the use of a ball joint, so you also need to make sure any bolts between trailer cycle frame and towbar are done up tightly.

USEFUL EXTRAS

Most trailer cycles can be detached in seconds without tools, leaving the hitch or rack on the towing bike. If you buy an extra rack or hitch, you can readily swap the trailer cycle between bikes. So, for example, if you wanted to use a trailer cycle for the school run, one parent could drop off, the other pick up. The trailer cycle could be locked up at or near school in the interim.

Whatever attachment the trailer cycle uses, ease of removal must not compromise security. The hitch must not be able to come off the bike, or the towing arm from the hitch, by itself. Even if a quick-release comes loose, there should be some failsafe to stop it detaching instantly.

The use-life of your trailer cycle will be longer if it can accommodate a growing child. Some have handlebars that can be clamped further up the frame to suit a bigger child. You can also raise the saddle on any trailer cycle. If you're intending to use one for children of different sizes – for

example, sometimes carrying your five year-old, sometimes your seven year-old – then it makes sense to fit a quick-release seat binder bolt. This will enable you to adjust saddle height for each journey.

Six- or seven-speed gears don't add much to the cost of a trailer cycle and are well worth having. Your passenger can contribute more to the ride by pedalling on the flat and uphill. It's good practice for a child's own bike, too. If you get a single speed, the gear needs to be fairly low so that your child can help you by putting some power in when you most need it: going uphill.

A brake isn't necessary for the trailer cycle and could even be dangerous. Used at the wrong time, such as when you're not braking, the trailer cycle would skid. Your bike's brakes must be good, although you need to apply them progressively rather than suddenly if you're going down a steep hill, as the trailer cycle can shunt the towing bike.

If you're attaching a trailer cycle to the back of an already heavy bike, such as a tandem, it's worth adding a drag brake to the towing bike to help keep your speed under control during any long descents.

Make sure the towing bike has a rear mudguard, ideally with a mudflap, otherwise you'll spray road run-off into the face of your passenger. If there isn't a mudflap, fit a mountain bike-style down tube guard to the trailer cycle. The trailer cycle itself needs a mudguard too. If you go out at night, it must also be fitted with a red reflector

3.2 Trailer cycles

Trailer cycles allow children to join in the fun and help with pedalling. These riders are in a procession on the way to CTC's York Rally, which is why the rule on cyclists not riding more than two abreast has been waived. Photo: Peter Eland

Have regular stops for drinks and snacks. Even though you're doing most of the work, your child will tire before you do
Photo: Cycling Images

and a red rear light in order to comply with traffic law.

A slick or semi-slick tyre is better for the trailer cycle than a knobbly one, unless you really will be spending most off your time riding off-road. The lack of tread will enable it to roll easier.

Toe clips are useful to keep your child's feet on the pedals. That's better for balance and for fast pedalling, although it's not as important as it would be a tandem. A child can freewheel independently on a trailer cycle, so there isn't the risk that flailing legs will get whacked by pedals that you're still cranking around.

Some trailer cycles fold along the towbar or around the seat tube. This is handy for storage, especially in the back of car, although it will probably be too big to carry onto a train as luggage. Be prepared to book it on a train as a full-size bicycle instead.

A mirror lets you keep an eye on your passenger and on following traffic, as it does with a child seat.

ON THE ROAD
You can usually put panniers on the towing bike when you're using a trailer

3.2 Trailer cycles

cycle. It's unwise to put them on the trailer cycle itself, because the added weight here will compromise bike handling just as if you were towing a heavier child. Trailer tricycles are an exception and will easily carry a hamper-sized load between the rear wheels, given a suitable rack.

You can tow a trailer cycle behind a tandem even more easily than you

> "Most of the time you won't get much help in powering along, yet when your co-rider really pedals you will feel it"

can behind a solo bicycle. It upsets the handling less, because the trailer cycle passenger is a smaller fraction of the weight that's on the towing bicycle.

If you want to use a child-back tandem to tow a trailer cycle, you'll need to use a rack-mounted model. That's because the child's seat – and hence, seatpost – will be so low down that the rear wheel will get in the way of a seatpost-mounted towing arm.

You can't usually ride with a rear child seat and a trailer cycle attached to the same bike. It is possible with the Roland Add+bike (from £215, www. bikesandtrailers.com), which attaches the trailer cycle to the very back of a custom rack.

From a handling point of view, this is worse than having the pivot above the towing bike's rear axle, but it's

not much further back and hence not much worse – and if you want trailer cycle plus child seat it's a compromise you'll need to make. It's still better than a seatpost hitch. On the subject of child seats: don't put one on the actual trailer cycle unless it's in place of, rather than as well as, the existing seat. Trailer tricycles work best for this.

Whatever kind of trailer cycle you use, you should instruct your co-rider to stay seated. The side-to-side lurch from your passenger pedalling standing up will severely affect your steering. Most of the time you won't get that much help in powering along. Yet when your co-rider does pedal in earnest, you will feel it and it does make a difference.

Do say how much you appreciate the help – it's good for their morale. Your child won't be able to keep pedalling hard for very long, so if you're on a big ride encourage him or her to conserve energy. Call for help when you see that hill ahead with a casual: 'Time for a turbo boost!'

Be aware that on longer rides your child will tire before you do, even though you're doing most of the work. Check morale and energy levels regularly by keeping a conversation going, and if necessary boost both with stops and snacks. Adults can feel themselves getting more tired; children can conk out in moments and suddenly be upset and tearful. They can even fall fast asleep as they're being towed along. On a trailer cycle, if they fall asleep they generally fall off…

Tandems

A TANDEM lets two riders of different abilities cycle together without anyone getting left behind. It's ideal for an adult and child. Cost is a lot higher than for a trailer cycle but it isn't simply a luxury version. A tandem can be combined with a child seat, child trailer, even a trailer cycle so that a whole family can ride together. Two adults can ride an adult tandem too, so it's something that can remain useful once the kiddy cranks are removed.

Most tandems have two seats, one behind the other, although there are versions with three seats (called a triplet) or even more. The front rider, called the pilot or captain, controls the steering, the brakes and the gears. The rear rider, called the stoker, helps to pedal. Because of the extra weight and power on a tandem compared to a solo bike, it's easiest to control if the heavier, stronger rider is the pilot – usually the man if husband and wife ride and always the adult if a child is on board.

A tandem is the most efficient family bicycle, bar none. Two adults can go faster than one adult on a solo bike, because, while you're doubling the power, weight isn't quite doubled (one tandem is lighter than two solos), and wind resistance stays almost the same. This gives the tandem a big speed advantage when you're going downhill, on the flat, or into a headwind. Even with an adult and a child on a tandem, speed is barely less than an adult cycling alone. If you're touring, it means you can travel further. If you're commuting, it means you have the option to step on it when running late!

Tandems don't go up hills as quickly as solo bikes unless the riders can manage to pedal out of the saddle in perfect unison. Some can; most can't. In that case, stick to pedalling while sitting down, shift to a lower gear, and accept that you'll make up ground when you get over the brow of the hill.

> "The main benefit of the child-back tandem over the adult tandem is that everything is scaled for your child from the start"

KNOW YOUR TANDEM

A tandem has to be built more sturdily than a solo bike, because it carries more weight over a longer frame. To stop it flexing from side to side as you pedal, an extra frame tube or two is usually added, running roughly along the bike's torsional axis. That's an imaginary line from the head tube, where the bike is steered, to the rear dropouts, which hold the rear wheel.

Some designs run a tube right along that axis, splitting it into an extra set of seat stays to reach the dropouts.

Some run a tube from the head tube to the rear bottom bracket instead, and there are other variations on this theme. A few designs ignore it entirely, but unless they incorporate massively oversized tubes the frame will flex with every pedal stroke. The heavier the riders – particularly the stoker – the worse the flex will be.

Tandems obviously have two sets of pedals, with an extra chain (called the timing chain) running between. On some tandems the timing chain is on the left, on some it's the right; either is fine. As the timing chain isn't kept in tension by a derailleur, another method is needed to stop it from going slack. This is achieved using an eccentric bottom bracket.

Inside a bigger outer shell, the actual bottom bracket is offset in a circular housing. Rotating the housing changes the position of the bottom bracket – a bit like the orbit of a coupling rod where it's fixed to a steam engine wheel. This scope for adjustment allows you to take up the chain tension. Bolts on the outer shell allow the housing to be held in position when the chain is adjusted.

A tandem's gearing is much like a solo bike's, except that the range ought to be greater. Ideally a tandem needs gears that go as low as a mountain bike's. It's harder to dance gracefully on the pedals to get a tandem uphill

Toe clips keep feet on the pedals, and so prevent any accidents with pedals spinning back round and hitting a child's leg
Photo: Cycling Images

A child-back tandem slopes down from front to back to fit both riders. Photo: Cycling Images

two adults ride tandem, the stoker often controls the drag brake (or other third brake). With a child on the back seat, the pilot operates the lot.

Tandem wheels need to be stronger. How much stronger depends on you and your stoker's weight. Some child-back tandems come with solo bike wheels, which is fine when you consider that an average adult plus one child only weigh the same as a heavy adult who might otherwise ride on the same wheels on a solo bike.

More spokes make the wheel stronger, of course, and even on a child-back tandem 36 spokes (also used on solos) will be better than 32. Tandem hubs and rims are available that take 40 or even 48 spokes per wheel. That provides valuable insurance against wheel damage if the tandem will be carrying more weight, whether in the form of heavy touring loads or a second adult. It's particularly worthwhile in 700C wheels, which are about 10 percent weaker than 26-inch wheels.

A tandem's tyres also need more pressure, to cope with the greater weight. Inflate them to the top end of the pressure rating on the tyre sidewall, even for a primary school-age stoker, and expect to exceed it with an adult stoker. (Don't worry: the tyres won't explode!)

A tandem can only carry the same number of panniers as a solo bike, so if you plan to take yours touring (or even shopping), make sure there are eyelets to fit a carrier rack at the front as well

as efficiently as a solo, and pedalling while sitting down requires lower gears. Conversely, it also wants gears that go as high as those on road racing bikes, so that you can take advantage of a tandem's superior power-to-wind-resistance downhill or on the flat. High gears aren't so important, however, because you can always just coast coming down.

Reliable brakes are vital. For an adult and child, a V-brake front and rear is sufficient. If you're also carrying luggage or towing a trailer, it's worth adding a drag brake – a kind of hub brake that's designed to be held on during a long or steep descent to slow you down rather than stop you. When

as at the rear. You'll need it. If you're camping, you may need a luggage trailer as well.

CHILD-BACK TANDEMS

A child-back tandem is made specifically for an adult pilot and a child stoker. The top tube slopes down steeply from front to back, so that you can both have your saddles at the right height. Bike length is less too, since a child doesn't need or want the same reach to the handlebars as an adult.

To an extent, a child-back tandem can grow with your child. A long seatpost is required, of course. Also useful is a telescoping stem for the stoker handlebars, so they can be moved further away as the years pass. Some tandems have 'double drilled' cranks. That is, there are two pedal holes in each crank: one closer to the bottom bracket axle for smaller children, and one further away for larger children. When the time is right, you unscrew and refit the pedals.

The main benefit of the child-back tandem over the adult tandem is that everything is scaled for your child from the start; you don't have to customise it. With the rear saddle so low down, your child will be able to get on and off without your help, too. Since the whole bike is a bit smaller, it's a little easier to live with than an all-adult tandem: easier to store and easier to get in or on a car.

A few custom frame builders are well known for their tandems and will readily make child-backs for a four-figure sum. Names to put into Google include: Longstaff Cycles, Bob Jackson Cycles, Roberts Cycles, and Mercian Cycles. For rather less outlay, you can get an off-the-peg child-back tandem. Thorn's Voyager (from £799) and Explorer (from £999) are great bikes for the price. Both are 26-inch wheel, steel-framed touring/utility tandems with slick tyres and decent quality mountain bike gearing. The Explorer's equipment is a bit better, and it comes with mudguards and a rear carrier rack. (See www.thorncycles.co.uk to find out more.)

Some tandems aren't made for a child stoker but would nevertheless fit because the seat will go low enough for a child to reach the pedals. The reach may be too great, in which case you will need a longer or telescoping stoker stem. Adult cranks are too long for children. An engineer who is able to cut down cranks to suit a child (see Chapter 3) can alternatively drill another pedal hole, which will allow two pedal positions – adult or child.

The Orbit Libra (£795, from www.tandems.co.uk) will fit a child stoker as well as an adult. An even more interesting option is the Bike Friday Family Traveller, a small-wheeled tandem that fits a child or adult stoker – and packs up into a couple of suitcases! The Bike Friday Family Triple Traveller is a three-seater version of the same bike. The middle seat is meant for a child and the rear for an adult or a child. You can only get such bikes to order in the

3.3 Tandems

UK. Try contacting www.foldingbikes.
co.uk and expect to pay around £2000,
depending on the exact specification.

ADAPTING AN ADULT TANDEM
Lowering the child down to the pedals
via a child-back tandem isn't the only
option. If you've already got an adult
tandem – or would prefer to buy one
so that you can convert it back again
when your child is bigger – the pedals
can come up to reach the child. So
long as you've got a good level of
mechanical competence, this is a
conversion you can do yourself. If not,
it's a job for your local bike shop.

What you need are kiddy cranks.
They are: a bottom bracket that bolts
to seat tube under the child's saddle; a
child-sized chainset; an extra timing
chain; and an extra chainring for the
tandem's drivetrain to link the child's
chain into the loop.

You could saw up an old bike to get
the bottom bracket. An easier way
to is to buy it: St John Street Cycles
(www.sjscyles.com) sell a kiddy crank
seat tube block for £50. Get yourself
a 110mm chainset while you're at
it (£20). You'll then need to add a
chainring to the tandem's main drive,
ideally no bigger than the child's or
you'll spin their legs like egg whisks.

It's easiest to add a chainring to the
right-hand side of the pilot's chainset
– using a new single ring right-hand
crank if the timing chain is on the
left, or a new double- or triple-ring
crank in place of the existing single
if the timing chain is on the right. It's

An adult tandem can be adapted for a child using kiddy cranks
Photo: Cycling Images

also possible to run the child's timing
chain to the pilot's left-hand crank or
to the left-hand stoker crank; the latter
is neatest. Get a tandem specialist to
advise – try www.tandems.co.uk,
www.longstaffcycles.co.uk, or
www.sjscyles.com. Once you've
bought a new adult crank and a new
chain or two, the conversion will cost
something over £100 – more if you use
more expensive components.

That's not quite it. You also need to
let your child reach the handlebars. A
long stoker stem and backswept stoker
bars is one option (around £80, from St
John Street Cycles). Another solution
requires a bit of DIY but arguably
works better for smaller children.

You will need: two pairs of drop handlebars; an extra stoker stem; two broom handles; lots of handlebar tape. Fit one pair of drop bars in the normal stoker stem, upside down, bar ends pointing backwards. Fit the other stoker stem pointing back from the child's seatpost, and in that fit the other pair of drop bars, also upside down but with the ends facing forwards. Saw down a broom handle so that it is several centimetres longer than the distance between the bar ends and wedge one end in each bar end, if necessary wrapping the broom in insulation tape to provide a tighter fit. Repeat with the other handle. (Your broom handles need to be roughly the right diameter. Take your drop bars to the hardware shop to check.) When you've done this, tighten all bolts and wrap the lot in handlebar tape. Your child will have handlebars all down each side and can hold on anywhere.

As your child grows, you can lower the kiddy crank attachment block down the seat tube and/or raise the saddle. And one day you can remove the whole caboodle and be left with a standard tandem.

CAN YOU RIDE TANDEM?

Riding a tandem is easier than riding a solo bike plus trailer cycle. The long wheelbase of a tandem makes is very stable, although the slightly bus-like cornering at slow speed takes some getting used to. There is very little 'tail wagging dog' as the child's weight on a tandem is between the steering bike's axles rather than way behind them, as on a trailer cycle. The restriction on weight only exists insofar that the pilot be heavier than the stoker – and even that's not vital.

The stoker has to trust the pilot completely and not try to steer the bike

"Talking together is easier on a tandem because you're so much closer together, so the ride is more social"

or tense up. That's more of a problem with adults than it is with children, who are both more trusting and a lot lighter! Once you're moving both riders are literally chained together and have to pedal simultaneously – even if that means you pedalling and dragging the stoker pedals around too. Inexperienced adult tandem riders may struggle to synchronise their pedalling efforts effectively.

Again, it's easier with a child stoker. Since you're so much bigger and stronger, you set the tempo and your son or daughter can join in or go through the motions as desired. The thing to watch for with a child stoker is his or her feet coming off the pedals. If you don't notice immediately, the pedals will come round again and whack dangling legs. Use toe clips to keep little feet in place.

The hardest part of tandem riding is starting and stopping, particularly for two adults. To get on, the pilot straddles the bike, feet on the floor, holding the brakes on. Leave the left-hand pedals at the bottom of the stroke, so that the stoker can use the rear left pedal as a mounting step to get onto the saddle and ready to go. This ensures the stoker won't spin the pedals backwards when stepping on, which could spin one of front pedals into one of the pilot's shins. Ouch.

With the stoker on board, you can roll the bike forward to put the right-hand pedal over the top of the stoke, ready to tread down onto, setting off and simultaneously rising up onto the pilot's saddle. That's the theory. Two adults will need some kind of signal to start pedalling simultaneously. With a child stoker, it's easier: you can just announce you're setting off and go – you'll have enough mass to get the tandem rolling by yourself.

This procedure works with a child stoker who is tall enough to get onto a child-back tandem and able to worm feet into toe clips unaided. If you've got a smaller child or a taller bike such as an adult tandem with kiddy cranks, it's a bit more complicated, because you have to get your child on first. It's much easier if the tandem has a drag brake – which can be left switched on – and a rear carrier rack. You can then put the drag brake on, straddle the rear rack, and hold the bike steady with your thighs. Lift your stoker onto the saddle and slot feet into toe clips. Then, never forgetting to hold onto some part of the bike at all times, you

A tandem-style eccentric bottom bracket, here on a solo bike
Photo: Cycling Images

need to work your way to the front and step over the top tube. Do not swing your leg over your saddle: you will kick your stoker in the head.

Alternatively, you can straddle the front of the bike, facing towards the back and holding the top tube between your thighs. Again, switch on the drag brake if you have one. Now reach down and lift junior onto the saddle. To get going, you just have to step back off the bike and back onto it facing the right way, at all times holding some part of the bike such as the pilot's saddle and/or handlebar.

To get off, you put your feet down and reverse whatever procedure you used to get you both on.

With a double child-back triplet one parent can take two children out for the day. Three children? Add a rack-fitting trailer cycle!
Photo: Cycling Images

TANDEM TIPS

Talking together is easier on a tandem because you're much closer together, so the ride is more social. Plus it's more egalitarian: a child on a tandem is more part of a partner in the cycling experience than the trailer cyclist, who really is 'tagging along'. The general tips for riding with a trailer cycle also apply to tandems. Keep an eye out for your stoker getting drowsy – perhaps with a mirror?

There are lots of combinations to get families mobile. Tandem plus trailer cycle. Adult-sized triplet with kiddy cranks in the middle and a child seat behind the rear stoker... I used a Thorn 'Me'n'U2' double child-back triplet.

By the time you read this, this out-of-production bike may be available again; contact www.sjscycles.com. If not, they may have reconditioned ones for sale, and they will certainly make a custom one if you're prepared to pay.

Tandems are harder to transport than solo bikes. You'll need a special roof-rack adapter for your car, such as the Pendle Tandem Carrier (£167, www.tandems.co.uk). Some intercity trains will accept tandem bookings; most trains won't.

If you want more information or inspiration, consider joining the Tandem Club (£10, www.tandem-club.org.uk), which was founded by CTC members in 1971.

Special needs

ANYONE CAN CYCLE. Bicycles and tricycles can be built or adapted to suit virtually any requirement. The whole point of a cycle is to amplify your own efforts to make you move more efficiently. If a standard bicycle doesn't suit, you or your child just need something different. Able-bodied cyclists often customise cycles to their own requirements, and some have specially-made bikes. It's the same process, taken slightly further, with special needs.

Disabilities are by their very nature individual. To give you an idea of scope, however, here are just some of the special needs that can be met: blind or visually impaired, multiple sclerosis, Down's Syndrome, muscular dystrophy, dwarfism, thalidomide disability, amputee, limited leg movement, paraplegia… It's not uncommon for people who can't walk, at least not unaided, to cycle.

Many special needs can be met with solo cycles, often tricycles. Prices are a lot higher than for conventional machines, but the sense of freedom and independence they can grant to someone can't be overstated. When you're cycling in a family group, tandems offer more options for able-bodied and disabled to ride together.

Conventional adult or child-back tandems are, with no or minimal modification, suitable for some disabled stokers. Since only the pilot steers, it's no problem if the stoker is partially sighted. Blind stokers can be better than sighted ones, in fact, since they don't try to control the bike. It makes even more sense to fit toe clips or clipless pedals to prevent feet slipping. Tandems are also suitable for stokers who lack the strength or traffic-awareness to cycle alone.

THREE WHEELS GOOD
On a tricycle of some kind, virtually any disability can be catered for, from an inability to balance through to an inability to pedal. Seating, steering, gearing, and even braking can all be altered to suit.

An upright tandem tricycle is a good solution if you have a stoker with some balance problems and you want a more efficient ride than you'd get with Pashley's trailer tricycles. Your stoker won't upset the ride like they might on a bicycle tandem. Tandem trikes are expensive, but if you're buying it for a disabled user you should be exempt from VAT. Longstaff Cycles are the best-known tandem trike makers, and have lots of experience with disabled cyclists (www.longstaffcycles.co.uk). Expect to pay from £4,000.

For more serious balance problems, a recumbent tandem trike – which has a sun lounger-style seat rather than a saddle to perch on – is a better solution. It also adds the option of hand cranks instead of pedals for pilot or stoker. Expect to pay around £6,000 for a Greenspeed tandem recumbent trike, and a bit more for one with hand cranks in place of pedals. See www. wrhpv.com. The Hase Pino tandem (below) sits just one of the riders on a recumbent seat.

If you want your child to be independent some of the time and cycling with you at other times, two KettWiesel trikes (from £1388 each, www.londonrecumbents.co.uk and www.hase-bikes.com) are a versatile solution. They can be ridden coupled together or separately, and the there is a host of adaptations available, including children's versions, hand cranks, lap and waist belts, footplates, pedals with calf support, a carrier for crutches, a hydraulic back pedal brake, long handlebars for riders with short arms – and more.

Stability via three wheels, a back rest and a belt. Tandem trikes and trailer trikes can be adapted like this. Photo: Cycling Images

CYCLING WITHOUT PEDALLING

Not everyone can pedal or use hand cranks. There are cycles available where only you pedal and your passenger simply enjoys the ride.

From the same people as the KettWiesel, The Hase Pino is a combined upright-recumbent tandem, with the rear rider on a saddle and the front rider on a recumbent seat. The rear rider pilots. Both get a great view and can talk very easily. Usually both of you pedal, and there are adapters to fit a child on the front. For a non-pedalling passenger you could fit foot/leg rests. A lap and chest belt are also available. Prices start at £2,200.

The Christiania trike (see Chapter 2) is available with a cargo box designed to accommodate a wheelchair user. The front of the box drops down to form a ramp. Or there's the Duet Wheelchair Tandem (also from London Recumbents, prices from £3125). This has the same wheel layout as a box trike, with two at the front, except that front section *is* a detachable wheelchair. When it forms part of the tricycle, the wheelchair is tilted backwards to provide a more secure seat.

Both the Christiania trike and Duet are available with electric assistance if you need a bit more power to get around with your passenger.

MOST CHILDREN CAN LEARN to ride a bicycle between the ages of three and six. Even before that they can enjoy getting around on wheels of their own using a tricycle, push-along, or scooter. And they do enjoy it: apart from walking, it's the only practical alternative means a child has for getting about. It's different, it's faster, and it's fun.

A child's first set of wheels will likely be a push-along. As it won't require balancing like a two wheeler even small toddlers can paddle one around on the carpet or in the backyard. The first pedalled machine will typically be a tricycle, with solid tyres and the pedals directly mounted to the larger front wheel.

It might seem a step back to go from that to a two wheeler without any pedals at all. Nevertheless, that is the next step – whether it's a scooter, a hobby-horse-style learner bike, or a small bicycle with its pedals removed. That's because the secret of bicycling is not pedalling but balancing. Some people prefer trikes – there is even a Tricycle Association (www.tricycleassociation.org.uk) – and some can ride only trikes. Most children, however, want to get rid of their third wheel; it's a rite of passage of sorts.

A child who can already ride a two-wheeled scooter can very quickly learn to ride a bicycle. A child who has a bicycle with stabilisers can't begin to learn until the stabilisers are removed, because they effectively turn the bicycle into a tricycle. Balancing is a skill that can't be done for you and the only way to learn it is to do it. Once a child can balance on two wheels, everything else is an incremental step – braking, pedalling, and later on changing gear.

The first proper bike will likely be one with 12, 14 or 16-inch wheels and one gear. After that, your child will progress through bikes with 20 and 24-inch wheels before being big enough, around the age of 12 or 13, for a bike with 26-inch wheels, such as a Small or Extra-Small sized adult's mountain bike.

It can be tempting to buy the biggest bicycle that your child can sit on. Try to resist this. Bikes aren't like school jumpers that can be worn baggy and 'grown into'. A bike that's too large will be awkward to ride at the very least, and at worst could cause an accident. Out-grown bikes can be handed on to siblings or sold second hand.

Training wheels

NO, NOT STABILISERS. By training wheels I mean the various cycles and push-alongs that pre-school children can enjoy before their first bicycle. Primarily play equipment, such devices can be used for trundling to a corner shop or nursery with a parent.

PUSH-ALONGS

Push-alongs usually have plastic frames and plastic wheels with plain bearings. Even a cheap one should last long enough for one toddler to outgrow it. If you want something that can be handed on to a sibling – or are buying items for a playgroup – it's worth investing in something more durable.

A good choice is the Puky Whoosh (£45, www.amba-marketing.com), which is like a tricycle with two front wheels and no pedals. It suits riders from 18 months. Winther do something similar called the Push-Bike for One. Winther's excellently named Ben Hur trike is even better. It takes one or two riders; the second stands on a footplate at the back. It costs around £80 for the Mini-Viking version (www.a-winther.com).

TRICYCLES

Lots of pedal tricycles are plastic, too. The problem with them is that, when there's a plain bearing like a plastic sleeve at a pedal axle, it tends to break. A metal tricycle will last longer. If it has ball bearings for the front wheel, headset and ideally rear wheels, everything will spin or turn more easily, without going wobbly or falling apart. Look for wide-set rear wheels for stability, and scope for a growing rider to sit further back to pedal.

Puky and Winther (see above) both do good trikes. Another great one is the aluminium-framed Li'l Giant (£75, www.giant-bicycle.com): it has all the features you'd want plus a ding-a-long bell, which should alert pedestrians before their ankles are bashed. Low-rider trikes sit the child in a bucket seat nearer to the ground, with the wheels wide set to the side of the seat. The advantage of this set-up is that it's very difficult to fall off, and even if your child does there's little distance to fall before hitting the ground. The same criteria for buying upright trikes applies. Winther's Easyrider (around £120) is a good one.

Chain-driven tricycles for children aged three to five are rare nowadays. Mission Cycles make some, but my favourite is the Pashley Pickle – a traditional trike with pneumatic tyres, a front brake, a full chaincase and a bell (£295, www.pashley.co.uk).

SCOOTERS

A learner bike is a normal bicycle minus the pedals and the rest of the drivetrain. A scooter is a learner bike minus the saddle. Is it still in the bicycle family? It doesn't matter. To ride one, a child still has to be able to balance and steer. Some scooters even have a hand or foot brake, which teaches one more skill that's useful on the bike. Because it's like riding a bike, riding a scooter isn't easy at first. Under-threes might struggle.

Any two-wheeled scooter, even a mini scooter with skate wheels, will subtly teach the basics of balance. Bigger wheels with pneumatic tyres are a bit better. Once again, Puky and Winther have a number to choose from, from about £60 upwards. Mission Cycles also have some good ones (see www.missioncycles.co.uk).

LEARNER BIKES

Learner bikes hark back to the original bicycle: the 1817 'running machine'

A two-wheeled scooter like this one from Winther teaches balance and steering and makes learning to ride easy

of Baron Karl von Drais. Your child 'paddles' along the floor using alternate feet and can lift both to coast – essentially cycling.

There are lots to choose from nowadays, suiting children aged two to five. Look for a comfortable and slightly concave saddle to prevent your child from slipping forward. Handlebars and wheels should turn easily and freely, which they'll do best with ball bearings. Pneumatic tyres are lighter, more comfortable and roll better, especially over bumps. Handgrips must be secure, and a footplate means that legs need not flail during extended coasting.

The best looking learner bikes are the lovely wooden Likeabikes (from £115, www.likeabike.co.uk). But I'd pick the Puky Learner Bike Original with Brake (£80) as it's cheaper, ticks all the boxes, also comes with a footplate, brake, and kickstand. The bulb-ended handgrips won't jab a child's body in the event of a fall, and help keep hands from slipping off the ends. The Islabikes Rothan (£75, www.islabikes.co.uk) is another good one. If you're on a budget, the Joey Running Bikes Ratz-Fraz costs just £40 (www.joeyrunningbikes.com) and is more than adequate.

The more proficient your child becomes on his or her learner bike, the more he or she will be able to push off and coast along. In fact, those long strides on a learner bike, with both feet in the air, are the first steps in learning to master the magic skill...

Teach your child to ride

THERE ARE A NUMBER OF WAYS to learn to ride. One of them – you may remember yourself – involves stabilisers on a little bike, stabilisers being removed, and dad running along behind you holding the saddle, then letting go… only for you to panic, wobble, and crash into a hawthorn hedge. It does work – eventually. Plenty of us riding around today are the proof. There are ways that are easier, quicker, and less painful.

First off, don't put your faith in stabilisers. They don't help. They don't do any harm, they just turn the bicycle into a sort of tricycle, which your son or daughter might quite enjoy pedalling around. But your child won't actually begin to learn how to cycle until the stabilisers are removed. That's because the key component of cycling is balancing, which you can't learn if something – or someone – is holding you up.

A PROPER BIKE

Children develop differently so it's impossible to give an exact age when they're ready for a proper bicycle. However, children can usually learn to ride a two-wheeler at the age of three. Almost all are capable of learning to ride by five or six. I can't stress this enough: it's much easier and much quicker if they've got experience of balancing and steering already, either from a scooter or learner bike.

In fact, you can go through 90 percent of the 'teaching to ride' drill using only a learner bike. If you will be using a normal bicycle, the first step, apart from discarding any stabilisers, is to turn the bicycle into a learner bike. Remove the pedals – not forgetting that the left-hand pedal unscrews clockwise – and wrap electrical insulation tape around the crank ends to cover up any sharp burrs and provide a bit of padding in case it connects with a leg or ankle.

Next, lower the saddle so that your child can put both feet flat on the floor. (If that's not possible, and if your child can't easily straddle the top tube with feet on the floor, then the bike is too big.) You now have a learner bike.

Dress your child in such a way that grazes are unlikely in the event of a fall. Learning to ride a bike doesn't necessarily involve falling off. However, it can happen. Falls that hurt can magnify the fear of 'leaping into the dark' that learning to balance represents. So to prevent scrapes, it's better if your child wears a long-sleeve top and long trousers – fastened back at the ankle with an elastic band if they could catch on anything. While not essential, a helmet (see Chapter 4) and child-sized cycling mitts can be also useful to prevent scrapes to the head or hands. The Polaris Controller Mitt (£7.49, www.polaris-apparel. co.uk) comes in a variety of child sizes.

Paddling along the floor and coasting down gentle slopes is the best way to learn to cycle, using a learner bike like this Likeabike Jumper or a small bicycle with its pedals removed. Photo: Likeabike

4.3 Teach your child to ride

Remind your child how the bicycle's steering works – that if you point the handlebars that way, you go that way. Show your child how to work at least the front brake. It's more powerful than the rear and requires less hand strength to operate. Moreover, the right is usually the dominant hand. Get your child to demonstrate using the brake, so that you can be secure in the knowledge that he or she can reach and use the lever. Normally it's a bad idea to depend on the front brake alone; at walking pace, it doesn't really matter. If your child is on a learner bike without a brake, stopping means using shoe leather. In this case, it's important for stability that your child puts both feet down to stop. Again, spell this out.

TIME TO RIDE

Now find a gentle slope. Tarmac footpaths away from through-traffic are good, as are empty driveways, as you don't get the bumps between slabs like you do with paved paths. Avoid parked cars: a shouting neighbour whose car has just been hit will distress your child. Grass hurts less if your child falls, but an uneven surface makes a fall more likely.

Set junior astride the bike and walk 5-10 metres down the gentle slope. Ask your child to push off and steer towards you. To begin with, this may mean them scooting all the way towards you, feet alternately on the floor. That's fine. As your child's confidence grows, encourage coasting – keeping the feet in the air for longer periods between dabs.

It can go wrong at the coasting stage. Your child may look at the floor or off to one side. This will result in a wobble and maybe a fall. On a bike, you go where you look. That's why you're standing in front and not behind: you're the target. If you're behind, your child may panic, look around, and crash. Stay in front and repeat the phrase: 'Look at me!' If your child is looking at you, he or she will instinctively steer towards you. And if anything does start to go wrong, you can take a few steps forward and grab the handlebars to prevent a fall.

Once your child can coast for a short distance, encourage him or her to coast for longer – which may mean pushing off, then coasting, then pushing off again if the slope's gradient doesn't provide enough momentum. So that you're not too far away, it can help if you walk or trot backwards a few metres in front of your child, again repeating the mantra 'Look at me.' (Don't forget to glance backwards so that you don't fall over!)

If two adults are available, one can walk behind – silently and not holding bike or child – while the other stays still further away, calling out 'look at me'. The advantage of this is solely for the adults involved: it means no one has to trot backwards.

Encourage your child to slow down and stop using the brake(s) before putting the feet down. But be ready to step in and offer support in the event of any absent-mindedness. Above all, be sure to let your child know how well he or she is doing. Cycling is not innate: it's a tricky skill to learn, and while we never forget it we do forget how hard it seemed when we were small. If there's any frustration, tiredness or tears, then simply stop. There's always tomorrow. It might be that your child will learn in under an hour, or it might take several hours spread over several days.

REFIT THE PEDALS

Sooner or later, your child will master the art of coasting. He or she will be able to push around, steer, brake, and freewheel for as long as the momentum lasts. With the magic skill of balancing a bicycle already in the bag, your child is almost done.

To turn this into cycling, you just need to refit the pedals. Leave the saddle where it is for now, nice and low. Adults and older children won't want the saddle set this low, but for small children it's very important that they can still get both feet down on the floor easily.

Go back to your gentle slope and repeat the ride-towards-you sessions, only instead of coasting this time encourage your child to lift the feet, put them on the pedals and pedal. Again, you may find your child looks down. Repeat the mantra: 'Look at me.' It's better for your child to coast under control, initially unable to find the pedals, than to look down and pedal into a hedge. Pedalling does affect the

steering of a bicycle, so to begin with just practise getting the feet on the pedals and coasting. Then you can introduce pedalling.

As your child's confidence grows, get him or her to pedal along on the flat – towards you as you trot backwards. Repeat as necessary. Once this has fully sunk in, you can let your child ride without you as a target. Stay nearby, though. Don't just tell your child 'Remember to look where you're going'. That means essentially nothing to a four-year-old. Spell it out: 'On a bicycle, you go where you look. So look where you want to go'. Kids are smart and catch on quickly.

Once your child can coast confidently, refit the pedals and it should all be plain sailing. Photo: Cycling Images

Buying a bike for your child

BICYCLE PRICES don't simply scale down with size. Raw material savings are modest. A child's bike uses shorter lengths of tubing, but smaller components are not intrinsically cheaper. And unlike clothes, children's bikes aren't VAT-free. So how come most children's bikes are much cheaper? Because lots of them are Bicycle-Shaped Objects, offering the appearance of a mountain bike but none of its function. This stylish-looking oversize frame could be heavy mild steel instead of lightweight aluminium, and that suspension fork could move more fore and aft than it does up and down.

It's the same story as with cheap adult bikes only worse. Children's bikes more than any other are built down to a price – the kind of price that would buy just a couple of PlayStation games. You find these bikes in catalogues and toy shops – or skips, because cheap and nasty bikes don't last. They break down and are abandoned. A good bike will still be in use several Christmases later and can be handed down to a brother or sister. So its yearly cost can be a lot less, even if it's two or three times the price to begin with.

Children will tolerate, even enjoy, almost any bike. If you get them a good one, however, they'll keep using it after the initial thrill of having a new bike has faded. Good bikes get used, day in, day out, because they're a pleasure to ride. Bad bikes, on the other hand, slowly decay in sheds.

Decent children's bicycles aren't hugely expensive. You can get a good bike for a five-year-old for around £100, and a really nice one for a 10-year-old for £200-£250. That's no more than an Xbox 360, and a good deal less when you factor in the price of games. And which would you rather your child played with?

There are perfectly acceptable bikes available for less than this, of course, but with new bikes it means sorting the wheat from a much larger volume of chaff. Bargains are rare – unless you buy second hand.

The local newspaper adverts or eBay (www.ebay.co.uk) can yield good deals, if you know what you're looking for. If not, minimise the risk of buying a turkey by purchasing from keen cyclists. Cycling enthusiasts will probably have bought something decent in the first place and maintained it. The 'for sale' board on the CTC Forum (http://forum.ctc.org.uk) is a great first stop. Other UK sites (such as BikeRadar) and cycling magazines may also be useful.

A lightweight bike that fits and works well, like this one, is a much better buy than a similarly priced heavyweight with a cheap and nasty suspension fork and cheap cable disc brakes. Photo: Stockfile

Soho series from £350.00

FX series from £230.00

SU series from £350.00

The New 2008 Hybrid and City Bike line up from Trek

Derailleurs, Hub Gears, Singlespeed, V-brake, Disc Brake, Panniers, Mud Guards, Child Trailer, Commute or Coffee Shop Cruise. Whatever you need, whatever you want - there is a Trek Bike to fit into your life.

See the entire Trek 2008 range, and find your nearest dealer online at: **www.trekbikes.com/uk/en** Or call: 01908 282 626

WEIGHTY ISSUES

Size and weight need scaling down to suit a child. That sounds obvious but I've tested tiny bikes for seven-year-olds that were heavier than any of mine. Bike weight is always a bigger proportion of a child's bodyweight than an adult's, often as much as a half or a third instead of around a seventh. That only makes it even more important to reduce it. Weight impacts on the fun and manoeuvrability of a child's bike. Imagine strapping a couple of breeze blocks to your own bike. That's the kind of extra weight we're talking about, in relative terms, on some children's bikes.

> "As bikes get bigger and start to feature the kind of components you'd expect on an adult bike, so prices rise, too"

The trickledown of aluminium tubing into the lower price brackets means that many children's bikes are finally getting lighter. While aluminium isn't inherently better than steel, the way children's bikes are built nowadays – cheaply, sturdily, with over-size and odd-shaped tubes – it's a lot lighter. To check a bike's weight before you buy, you don't need to take a set of scales to the shop. Just pick the bike up. Then, with careful supervision, see how easily your child can lift it.

A QUESTION OF SCALE

Standard cycle components are made to fit the average sized man. Components for children's bicycles clearly need shrinking down to suit a smaller rider. Frames and wheels always are, to some extent. With other components it's hit and miss.

In particular, cranks are almost always too long. Over-long cranks are ungainly and inefficient. They force the bottom bracket to be higher off the ground to avoid pedal strikes, and this makes it harder to get a foot down from the saddle. As a rule of thumb children need cranks that are roughly one-tenth their overall height, just like adults. So a child 1.2 metres tall needs 120mm cranks.

You can get a more accurate figure using 20 percent of leg length instead. To measure that, don't use trouser size. Instead, subtract height when sitting against a wall from height standing against a wall. That's your leg length. A fifth of this figure is the required crank length. The cranks don't need to match to the exact millimetre but the measurement is a good guide. If in doubt, it's better to err on the short side than long. The problem is that most manufacturers fit children's bikes with, at best, whatever cranks ought to be on the next bike size up.

The handlebar should be narrower than the 60cm riser handlebar that you might use on a mountain bike, but this isn't so critical. A wide handlebar is good for control and in a fairly upright riding position isn't usually

4.4 Buying a bike for your child

Older children don't have to be able to put both feet flat on the floor like learners, but should still be able to get one foot down easily
Photo: Cycling Images

uncomfortable. If it is, you can easily cut the bar shorter with a hacksaw.

Brake levers must be within easy reach and the brakes must be easily operable: children have much weaker grip strength than adults. Check that you can reach and work each brake with one little finger. Hydraulic disc brakes are best but cost too much to be fitted to anything but high-end children's mountain bikes. Smoothly functioning V-brakes are okay. Grip shift-style twist shifters require less thumb strength than Rapidfire levers, and younger children in particular seem to find them more intuitive.

One measurement that doesn't scale well to children's bikes is reach – the distance between the saddle and the handlebars. Most children are happier in a riding position that's both shorter and more upright than you would adopt, so they need the bars higher and closer. BMX handlebars are excellent on bikes with 20-inch or smaller wheels for that reason.

THE GROWING CYCLIST
Optimum bike fit comes by progressing in stages rather than fitting your child onto the biggest bike he or she can pedal. For safety's sake, your child must be able to get a foot down easily when sitting on the saddle – both feet for learners – and able to stand with both feet flat on the floor

Cranks are usually too long on children's bikes. These have been cut down to size by an engineer. Photo: Dan Joyce

than another's.

You don't have to buy your child a bike at every wheel size, although that would be ideal. Just be aware that a bike with significantly bigger wheels than those your child is used to will make bike control harder. While a larger wheel will roll over bumps better, it will also be heavier and the steering will be less responsive. The reach to the bars will likely be greater and the bottom bracket will be higher.

Conversely, there will come a time when your son or daughter is just too big for that old bike. Two or three years per bike is fairly typical. You can recoup some of your costs by selling on a used bike, or you can extend its use-life by handing it down to a sibling. Avoid the temptation to buy something cheap and nasty: a bike that barely gets used isn't a bargain, however inexpensive it is.

while straddling the top tube in front of the saddle. Otherwise there's an accident there waiting to happen.

Children's bikes can be divided by wheel diameter into five sizes: under 16 inches, 16 inches, 20 inches, 24 inches and 26 inches. These sizes correspond to approximate age ranges, but you might find your child is ready for (or outgrows) a given size a year or two earlier. Also, bear in mind that the use of different frame designs mean that one manufacturer's 24in-wheel bike might be slightly bigger or smaller

ONE BIKE FOR EVERYTHING

While keen adult cyclists may have several bikes, most children will at any given time have just one. The ride to school bike, the off-road bike, the bike for cycling in the lanes – they're one and the same. No bike is best at everything so there will be compromises to make somewhere. Those may include balancing what your child wants with what your child actually needs.

This isn't an issue with smaller bikes. A decent pavement bike will do everything its five-year-old owner will ask of it. As your child starts to use the bike for longer and different journeys – an issue for bikes with 24in and larger wheels, typically – the need for a bike that's versatile enough to tackle all those trips becomes greater.

A hybrid would be ideal, as the name suggests, but there are few – if any – made for children. The next best option is some kind of mountain bike, which your child will be happier with in any case because off-road bikes are more fashionable. Even those that won't go off-road can be good general-purpose bikes. The bike needs to be versatile. It's a given that it will go off-road, assuming it's not a BSO. But are there eyelets to fit mudguards for weekday street use? Could you fit a rear carrier rack for a school bag, or for that cycling holiday?

Most children own one bike, so versatility is important
Photo: Cycling Images

This need for versatility will dictate some kind of hardtail – either with a suspension fork or a rigid fork. It's worth changing the tyres, or at least getting an extra pair. Knobbly off-road tyres might look cool but they are slow and hard work on tarmac.

You could fit semi-slicks – tyres with some tread but not the tractor tyre knobbles of true off-road tyres. The local bike shop may even be happy to swap them over at point of purchase. Semi-slicks will roll better on road and will still be okay off-road when it's dry. A more effective option, but one that's a bit more hassle, is to fit slick tyres to the bike for everyday use and then switch them for the off-road tyres the night before singletrack excursions.

AGES 3-5: SUB 16-INCH WHEELS
Low weight and correct proportions are the priorities for a starter bike, which will have 12 or 14in wheels. Gimmicks – for example, being overbuilt so as to look like a motorbike – are best avoided. Look for an upright riding position, courtesy of a BMX-style handlebar, a low stand-over height, and short cranks (90-100mm). Smooth pneumatic tyres roll better than knobbly ones or tyres that have been filled with foam. The wheels, bottom bracket and headset should all use ball bearings instead of stiff or sloppy plain bearings, where plastic turns on plastic.

Gearing will be single-speed, which is fine. The brakes should be easy to operate; once again do the little finger brake check. V-brakes are effective stoppers, but even better for a starter bike's rear wheel is a back-pedal brake. A rear brake takes more effort than a front brake due to cable friction and uses the (usually) weaker hand. Using the legs instead overcomes this, and pedalling back to stop is intuitive for a new cyclist. Stabilisers are common on bikes of this size; at some point, you'll want to remove these.

The best bike of this kind is Islabikes' Cnoc 14 (£110, www.islabikes.co.uk). It's scaled down perfectly for a small child, with 89mm cranks and a tiny front brake lever. The rear is a back-pedal brake, which gives more reliable stopping. Tyres are treaded for street riding and aluminium tubing keeps weight down to just 7.3kg (16lb).

Cheaper options won't be as light or as well made, yet serviceable bikes are available for under £50 if you shop carefully. The 14in-wheel bikes – branded Corky, Cheese and Laly La Jolie – from Decathlon (www. btwincycle.com) are a benchmark for value. Unlike most at this price, they use ball bearings and pneumatic tyres. Weight isn't bad either. With others, follow the 'keep it simple' maxim.

AGES 4-6: 16-INCH WHEELS
Taller or older children can perhaps go straight to a 16in-wheel bike from a learner bike. Like 12- and 14in-wheel bikes, all 16in-wheel bikes come with a single-speed gear. The chain stays are too short for derailleur gears to function properly, and they would only

confuse a young child in any case. As children of this age won't be riding far, a single gear is fine.

Requirements are much the same as the smaller bikes: low stand-over; ball bearings; pneumatic tyres; decent brakes. A low-ish bottom bracket will help your child get a foot down when

"Less is more when it comes to quality. Avoid full suspension entirely unless you're spending serious money"

sitting on the saddle – which, as he or she can now ride properly, you'll be gradually raising. Cranks should be 100-120mm but 125mm isn't too bad.

You sometimes see cheap bikes in this size range with nasty suspension or monolithic steel frames. Avoid. Features like this add unnecessary weight and very little else. As with adult bikes, the less you're spending the simpler the bike should be.

The Islabikes Cnoc 16 is the best of the bunch. It's essentially the same as the smaller Cnoc 14 (see above) but scaled up with larger wheels for a slightly older child. Several other manufacturers offer simple, aluminium-framed single-speeds at around the £100 mark. Ridgeback's MX16 (£110, www.ridgeback.co.uk) is a good one, with V-brakes front and rear. Cranks are only a little too long at 127mm. The similar Dawes Blowfish (www.dawescycles.com) is £100.

4.4 Buying a bike for your child

Proper bikes! The Islabikes Cnoc 14 (top) is a great starter bike for children aged 3 to 5. The Beinn 26 (below) suits 9-12 year olds
Photos: Islabikes

AGES 6-9: 20-INCH WHEELS

Gears are the obvious extra for 20in-wheel bikes. While single-speeds are still fine, a 3-speed hub gear is even better: it's easy to understand, easy to use, and hard to break. Hub gears are more expensive for manufacturers to fit, however, so 5 or 6-speed derailleurs are what you'll commonly find.

If the bike does have a derailleur, get a derailleur guard for those occasions when the bike is dropped on its side. A kickstand is useful, as young children aren't good at propping their bikes up. Look for easy-to-use shifters, like Shimano's RevoShift twistgrip. Cranks will, once again, be too long. You want 110-130mm; 140mm is too big but not ridiculously so.

Some 20in-wheel bikes come with a suspension fork, or even full suspension. There are two disadvantages with these: extra weight; and less money to go round elsewhere. If you're paying a large amount of money for the bike, then you may find that the suspension fork provided is adequate. However, rigid bikes will still give a better return for your money.

One of the better bikes available with this wheel size is also one of the simplest: the Trek Jet 20 (£140, www.trekbike.co.uk) is a BMX-style singlespeed with an aluminium frame and a back-pedal brake to supplement its hand brakes. (Yes, that's three brakes on one bike.) Cranks are 115mm. Despite the low stand-over height, it offers good growing room.

Islabikes have another great bike in this size, the Beinn 20 (£150), while Puky offer what's perhaps the ultimate street/touring/ride to school bike for younger children: the Crusader 20-3. It uses a 3-speed hub gear with a back-pedal brake and it's equipped with everything: mudguards, a carrier rack, even dynamo lighting. It's not cheap at £230 but isn't overpriced if your child will be doing a lot of utility cycling. See www.amba-marketing.com.

AGES 8-12: 24-INCH WHEELS

As bikes get bigger and start to feature the kind of components you'd expect on an adult bike, so price rises, too. Good quality 24-inch wheel bikes start at about £150. For that you can expect a light(ish) weight aluminium frame, aluminium alloy wheels, and brand name V-brakes.

Most mini-mountain bikes from the bigger name brands, including Specialized, Trek, and Giant, will have an 18 or 21-speed drive train and a cheap suspension fork; it may even work adequately.

A better option would be a lighter rigid bike with a wide-range 8-speed cassette and a single chainring: it's lighter, simpler, easier to use, and more durable. Most children under 10 only end up confused by a front derailleur and the bike invariably ends up with the chain on the smallest chainring and smallest sprocket, where it runs noisily and inefficiently.

Tyres will have off-road tread on most bikes. Children like the look of these but a set of semi-slicks would be a better compromise (see above). The cranks will again be too long: ideally you want 140mm, but could compromise at 150mm.

A few manufacturers offer road (racing) bikes in this size. As it's something of a niche market for English-speaking countries, the quality tends to be pretty good and the price high. Expect the components that you would expect, pound for pound, with an entry-level road bike: Shimano Sora gearing, aluminium frame, and so on. Also note that the shorter reach that children prefer requires a short stem and short reach, shallow drops.

Yet again Islabikes tick all the boxes, not only with the Beinn 24 (£200), but their smaller-than-usual 26in-wheel bikes, the Beinn 26 and drop bar Luath 26, which can be used for racing or touring. However, most of the big name brands do a reasonable hardtail mountain bike in this wheel size.

At £150, the Giant MTX 225 (www.giant-bicycle.com) is perhaps the best value. It uses a rigid fork, which saves both money and weight and sacrifices almost nothing in terms of function over a cheap suspension fork. Trek's Mt 220 (£200) is a good one, too: it uses cranks with two pedal holes so you can adjust the bike to suit a growing child's leg length.

Less is more. Trek's simple Jet 20 has one gear and a rigid fork, but as a street bike it's all that the average 6-9 year old needs
Photo: Trek

For children aged 12 and up, the next step is a small-framed adult mountain bike. This Specialized Hardrock Sport is a good one
Photo: Specialized

If you have a child who is an off-road fanatic, then high quality mountain bikes are also available in this wheel size. Kona (www.konaworld.uk.com) and Scott (www.scottusa.com) have several to choose from. These are real, scaled-down mountain bikes and so the price tags they carry fully reflect that: Kona's full-suspension Stinky 2-4 retails for £1,000!

AGES 12 AND UP: 26-INCH WHEELS
Children aged 12 or 13 are ready for a small-framed adult mountain bike with 26in wheels. Many manufacturers make frames down to 14 or 15in, and some do 12 or 13in frames. Trials fans and serious off-road riders may want the smallest frame for the extra clearance over the top tube, but most teenagers can go straight to 14 or 15in. (See Chapters 1 and 9 for more information on bike fit.)

Unless it's specifically aimed at children, resist the temptation to put your 9- or 10-year-old on a 26in-wheel bike just because he happens to be able to reach the pedals. He or she will be better off on a 24in-wheel bike, which will probably be lighter and will be easier to control than an adult bike.

The smaller bike should also have more kid-friendly components, such as cranks, whereas even a bike aimed at small adults will typically have average-sized adult cranks (170 or 175mm). Younger teens would be better off on 150 or 160mm.

The bike industry has been dragging its feet on the issue of crank length for years. So if you want cranks that are the right length for your 13-year-old, you'll probably have to have them shortened. It costs £40 from www.highpath.co.uk, where you can find more information about cycle transmissions in general.

An adult bike means adult prices: expect to pay from £200 for a sturdily built aluminium hardtail frame with a basic suspension fork. The closer

you spend to £300, the more likely it is the bike will have an adjustable suspension fork (for pre-load, at least), an 8-speed rear wheel (hence, 24 gears) and frame mounts for disc brakes. Some even come with cable disc brakes. Don't forget, though, that less is usually more when it comes to quality. Avoid full suspension entirely unless you're spending a serious amount of money.

Teenagers are acutely aware of peer pressure and will want a bike that's considered cool. Currently this seems to mean a mountain bike with a simple paint scheme – such as black, white, matt grey, silver, maybe red – and a chunky, dirt jump-style frame.

One good bike that fits these criteria is Specialized's Hardrock Sport (£300, www.specialized.com), which is available in both 12in and 15in frame sizes. The Saracen Mantra 1 (£300, www.saracencycles.com) is even burlier, which teenage boys will like, and is available in 15in. It comes with cable disc brakes too. Trek's frames go down to 13in, and anything from the 3900 up (£260) is suitable for regular off-road use as well as streets. The cheapest 'proper' mountain bike is probably Decathlon's Rockrider 5.2 (£199); the XS size is 15in.

Any cheaper and you're looking at street/towpath bikes. That's fine, too, so long as you accept that below £200 you're best off looking for a bike with no suspension, no disc brakes, fewer gears, and no gimmicks. That is, 'a bike' rather than 'an off-road bike'.

GOLDEN RULES FOR BUYING A KID'S BIKE

· Don't buy a bike for your child to grow into. For safety's sake, it must fit.
· Pick it up. Light weight is vital. Look for aluminium tubing or thin (i.e. cricket stump diameter) steel tubes.
· Be suspicious of suspension – especially at the rear of the bike. Cheap suspension is dead weight that serves no practical purpose.
· More gears are not better. Front derailleurs are superfluous until secondary school.
· Consider semi-slick tyres. Knobblies look cool but are hard work.
· Riding position should be fairly upright, with handlebars higher than the seat.
· Try the brakes using only your little finger. That's equivalent to a younger child's grip strength.
· If the cranks are much too long, see if they can be exchanged for the next size down at point of sale.
· Less is more. You never get something for nothing. Corners will be cut.

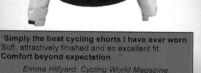

THE EXTRAS YOU NEED for cycling might begin and end with a pair of bicycle clips. It depends on what bike you'll be riding and where you'll be riding it. You can comfortably pedal a Dutch roadster a few miles in your best suit, but if you're going to ride 30 miles on a road bike then you'll be more comfortable in specialist cycle clothing.

You can select the bike to suit the clothing you'll be wearing, or you can select the clothing to suit the bike you'll be riding. The cyclist's 'uniform' of Lycra shorts, tight cycling jersey and a helmet is optional, however. It's no more necessary for, say, a short trip into town than a Formula One racing driver's outfit is for a car trip to Tesco.

If you're not going to ride in a sporty way then you don't need to dress like someone who's involved in cycle sport. It's like the difference between someone who is out for a jog and someone who is walking. Jogging equals sporty cycling equals special clothing. Walking is like cycling at an easy pace. It's easy, it doesn't make you sweat and you can wear pretty much anything you fancy. There are only two hard and fast guidelines for cycle clothing: you need to make sure it can't catch in the chain or the wheels; and you should wear whatever you're comfortable in – in both senses of the word.

Your freedom of choice in what to wear extends to cycle helmets. There's no legal obligation to wear one in Britain. You can wear one all of the time, just for certain situations, or never – it's up to you. Whether or not you do choose to wear one, you should be well aware of what they're designed for and what they're not designed for, so you can make an informed choice.

If you plan to use your bicycle as practical transport or at night then there are accessories you will need to buy. That's because bicycles are usually sold in Britain in a 'bare bones' format, without many of the things you'd take for granted in another form of transport, such as a car. For mountain bikes and road bikes, that makes sense. For utility bikes, it means you will have to shell out because your bike won't have a 'boot' for luggage and it won't have a lock to keep thieves at bay. Also, it will be illegal if you ride it at night, as it won't have lights.

The following chapter contains advice on all these optional extras, plus a few more that are well worth any cyclist owning.

What to wear

"DISTRUST ANY ENTERPRISE that requires new clothes," said American writer Henry Thoreau. In other words: if you can't do it in normal clothes then it isn't normal. Cycling has its own special clothes, and at the stretchy Lycra end of the spectrum you'd be hard pressed to say it looked normal – especially on anyone who isn't skinny.

Don't worry. Cycling gear is optional. If your journeys are short and/or slow, normal clothes are fine. The further and/or faster you ride, the more you'll benefit from switching to cycling clothes. It depends what bike you're riding, too – and in particular what the saddle is like.

SITTING COMFORTABLY

This section is about clothes rather than bicycle components, but it's difficult to avoid talking about the saddle when considering what to wear. The saddle is, literally, fundamental. Narrow saddles are for riding faster or further in cycling gear. Fatter ones are for riding shorter distances in normal clothes.

In padded shorts that narrow racing perch can be comfortable for hours – indeed, it will be more comfortable than a wide 'mattress' saddle. In normal clothes, that narrow saddle could be purgatory. Trouser seams can press painfully into your crotch. Jeans are about the worst, so if you want to wear them, get rid of the narrow saddle

and equip your bike with a wider saddle that's softer or sprung and that perhaps has a hole cut in the centre to relieve pressure.

Your bodyweight is meant to be carried on your 'sit bones' or ischial tuberosities when you sit on a bicycle saddle. Those are the bony bits at the bottom of your pelvis. Any saddle has to be at least as wide as your sit bones to be comfortable, which is why women's saddles are wider than men's – it's due to the wider pelvis.

Your weight isn't meant to be carried on the soft tissue of your undercarriage. There are a lot of nerves running there and if you compress them – or worse, garrotte them with a raised trouser seam – you can end up with pain or numbness in one of the last places you'd want it. If you ignore that warning sign then the problem may persist.

Finding a good saddle is worthwhile for any cyclist, but it's particularly important if there won't be a layer of padding between you and it. What works best will vary greatly from cyclist to cyclist – bottoms are as individual as their owners. Some cyclists swear by sprung leather saddles such as the Brooks B66 (£62, www.brooksengland.com). My town bike – which I do ride in jeans – is fitted with a Selle Royal Ergogel Men's Relaxed saddle (£35, www.extrauk. co.uk). Other people prefer the Terry

Liberator saddle range (around £35, www.terrybicycles.com).

For a sportier bike – a mountain bike or touring bike – you will likely want something narrower. See the other ranges from these companies, as well as Selle Italia's TransAm range and also the Rido saddle (£10, www.rido-cyclesaddles.com).

NORMAL CLOTHES

If you're not going to change the saddle on your 'normal clothes' bike, you may need to change your attire. Try tracksuit trousers or just lighter-weight trousers without thick seams – suit trousers are usually fine.

"Getting your core body temperature right is one of the trickiest jobs when you're wearing normal clothes"

If your bike doesn't come with a chainguard or chaincase then long trousers will need holding back at the ankle with a cycle clip or tucking into the socks to keep oil off them. Long skirts or dresses look very pastoral when riding a bike. They're not very practical unless the bike is equipped with a full chaincase and a skirt guard for the rear wheel to prevent any entanglements.

Trainers or street shoes are fine on flat platform pedals. Rubber pedal treads give good grip in the dry and won't scuff shoe leather. In the wet, they're slippier than studded or serrated metal pedals. It's possible to cycle in high heels, although you're better off changing into them afterwards and wearing trainers or pumps to ride in.

Whatever you wear, tie or tuck any laces in such a way that they can't snag on the chainring. This is vital for children on the back of tandems, where the drivetrain is inexorable, and even more vital on a fixed-wheel road bike where a jammed chain will instantly stop the back wheel.

Getting your core body temperature right is one of the trickiest jobs when you're wearing normal clothes. On a bike you generate more heat than you do when walking but you're subjected to more wind-chill, so you need to be windproof but not too insulated. In fact, you should be not quite warm enough when you set off, to prevent overheating a couple of miles further on. Be prepared to stop and shed a layer as you warm up or if conditions change. Similarly, be prepared to add a layer if you get off the bike and have to stand around in the cold.

Many coats are too warm for cycling and they tend to be cut wrong. They're too short in the back and arms because of the leaned-over position you adopt on most bikes. It's well worth considering getting a cycling jacket if you get no other cycling gear.

A windproof jacket made from a lightweight polyester, such as Pertex, is enough for the summer months and will shrug off light showers, while a breathable waterproof with a Gore-Tex membrane will vastly improve winter comfort. Expect to pay from about £30 for a windproof and around £100 for a truly breathable waterproof. Jackets that are waterproof and semi-breathable are cheaper – around £50. Good brands for jackets and other cycling clothes include Altura, Endura, Gill, Gore, Pearl Izumi and Polaris – who are also good for children's cycling gear (www.polaris-apparel.co.uk).

In winter, your hands and head – especially the ears – get cold due to wind-chill, so wrap up well. It's much worse than when you're walking. If you wear glasses, wear a cap when it rains to stop droplets getting onto your lenses and distorting your vision.

CYCLING CLOTHES

Padded shorts are standard-issue cycling kit. By default, they're black Lycra with a synthetic pad in the crotch. Cycling shorts are designed to be worn next to the skin without pants. It's more comfortable and the fact that you're not in sweaty skivvies reduces the chance of getting a rash. Racers sometimes pay over £100 for skin shorts, but good ones cost from about £20, and for light leisure use you can pick them up for as little as £6 from Decathlon. Note that men's and women's shorts have a different shaped shorts pad.

The disadvantage of Lycra shorts is that they're rather conspicuous off the bike and some folk feel self-conscious in them on the bike. You can wear them underneath other shorts or tracksuit trousers, or you can buy mountain bike baggies that do the same job. Some baggies come with a padded inner short, while with others you're expected to wear them over Lycra shorts. Expect to pay from £25 for baggies. In winter, you'll want leg- or knee-warmers to go with the shorts, or full-length Lycra cycling tights instead.

Cycling footwear is stiff and has cleats bolted to the sole. These clip into pedals a bit like ski boots into ski bindings. Treading down clips you in and twisting the foot sideways releases. You get a much more secure connection to the bike with these pedals, and better power transfer. Make sure the release springs are set up nice and loose to begin with, or else you'll end up lying on your side on the floor – still attached to the bike.

Shoes for road racers have cleats that stand proud of the sole and make you walk like a duck. Other shoes – branded off-road shoes but usable anywhere – have a recessed cleat so you can walk better. There are several different designs, and while cleat A won't fit in pedal B, pretty much any off-road cleat will fit any off-road shoe (similarly with road shoes). The cleats come with the pedals not the shoes, so you shouldn't have compatibility problems. Expect to pay from £20 for pedals and from £30 for the shoes.

For the top half, a stretch-fit synthetic jersey with pockets in the

Padded Lycra shorts (top) greatly improve comfort for sporty cycling but normal clothes (right) are fine for shorter trips. Cycling shoes (left) clip into matching pedals. These ones are for road racing. Photos: Dan Joyce and Cycling Images

back is typical. Often it will be worn over a wicking vest, which won't get soggy and clammy with sweat like cotton. On the top of that, if it's cooler, you can cheat the wind with a windproof jacket or a gilet, which is like a jacket minus the arms. Gilets cost much the same as jackets but are lighter and easier to stow in a cycling jersey pocket. Arm warmers and leg warmers are often used too, as they can be pulled on or off easily to suit changing temperatures. A combination of 'base layer' (vest), mid-layer (jersey) and outer layer (windproof) can be used all-year round. The winter option involves long sleeves and a snugger jersey.

Most cyclists wear padded mitts or gloves. These help prevent numbness in the hands due to compressed nerves and also protect the palms in the event of a fall. Headgear was traditionally a tight-fitting cotton cycling cap, which helps keep both sun and rain off and can be worn under a helmet. When it's really cold, the ears at least need covering – with a thin headband, beanie or balaclava if a helmet is to go over the top.

Many cyclists use clear or coloured wraparound glasses for cycling to keep out wind, dirt and insects. Prescription versions are also available – at a price. Optilabs are good value (www.optilabs.com).

Cycle helmets

Because cycling is an energetic activity, cycle helmets have to balance protection against the need for a low overall weight and good ventilation. Photo: Specialized

CYCLE HELMETS ARE designed to work as shock absorbers for your head. In a fall, the primary danger is not cuts or grazes to the scalp but the impact energy to your brain, which can slosh about your skull like you've been hit by a boxer. The helmet's job is to soak up as much of this energy as it can. It does this by compressing and crushing.

Cycle helmets are made mostly from a thick layer of expanded polystyrene (EPS), which is what does the crushing. This is covered with a plastic shell. That's meant to flex a bit on impact to distribute the shock through a wider area of EPS beneath and thereby soak up more energy. The shell should also skid on the ground.

To achieve a secure fit, a helmet cradles the back of the head with a harness that's adjustable with a ratchet or dial. Most have removable foam pads inside to improve comfort and fine-tune the fit. A buckled chinstrap keeps the helmet in place.

HELMET LIMITATIONS

The protective capabilities of cycle helmets are often exaggerated. A bicycle helmet is not a motorcycle helmet. Cycling is an energetic activity and for any helmet to be tolerable it must be light and well ventilated, or you would swiftly overheat. This limits the amount of protection available.

Cycle helmets are designed to protect the head from a fall from a bicycle at impact speeds of around 13mph where there is no other vehicle involved. That's all: simple falls and not at high speeds. They have extremely limited capacity in crashes involving motor vehicles, which account for 93% of serious cycling injuries and fatalities.

Nevertheless, a fall by itself – whether from a bicycle or not – can be serious. Helmets are of greatest use not as protection from traffic (where they are largely superfluous) but rather where falling is relatively common: among young or learner cyclists, for example; among mountain bikers, who ride on trickier terrain; and for cyclists on icy roads.

WEAR AND CARE

If you choose to wear a helmet, it's vital to wear it correctly. The helmet must protect the forehead. Don't wear it at a jaunty angle on the back of your head. The brim should be no more than a couple of fingers' width above your eyebrows and just visible in the top of your vision.

The straps should be fairly snug but not tight. The 'Y' of the straps should meet just under each earlobe. You should be able to get one or two fingers under the chinstrap (a useful

precaution while buckling a child's helmet to prevent pinched skin) so that it doesn't constrict your throat, but the strap shouldn't hang loose. It takes time to sort the strapping and cradle arrangement on a new helmet until it's just right. Take that time.

Of course, the helmet must fit to begin with. If it's loose on the head

> "If you choose to wear a helmet, it's vital to wear it correctly. Don't wear it at a jaunty angle on the back of your head"

then it could slip out of position. Try it for size in the shop, as you would with shoes. Some head shapes fit some helmets better than others.

Cycle helmets are designed to crumple. If you have a fall and bang it then you should replace it. Even if it's not visibly damaged there may be hairline cracks in the EPS that will prevent it functioning properly next time. Some manufacturers have a crash-replacement policy, which it's worth asking about in the bike shop. You send off your crashed helmet and they'll send you a new one.

Even if you don't crash your helmet it will still have a limited lifespan. Most manufacturers suggest five years – a fair guideline. Given a good degree of care a helmet might be used for longer. That means avoiding unnecessary knocks when it's being stored or carried, not putting anything heavy on top of it, and letting it dry out naturally if it gets wet. Those are all good precautions for a helmet in any case.

If your child is wearing a cycle helmet then make sure you remove it in any situation in which he or she can climb – such as at a play park. Children have been hanged by their helmet straps after falling and being held off the ground when the helmet has snagged on something.

WHICH HELMET?

Helmets are made from fairly inexpensive materials. A more expensive helmet won't necessarily offer better protection. What it will offer is lighter weight, better ventilation and more style.

Style is important in a helmet, insofar as a lack of style may be a barrier to wearing the helmet at all. Geeky looks are a particular issue with teenage children. Ventilation matters more the further and faster you ride. Racers need it; infants in child-seats don't. Weight is something all cyclists want less of, but with modern cycle helmets weighing around 250g-350g, it's not the issue it used to be.

The standard cycle helmet is an open shell formed of ribs and vents. Helmets for mountain biking have a detachable peak, which can be just as handy to keep the sun or rain out of your eyes for other types of cycling. Only for riding hard on drop handlebars is the peak a problem – you can't see where you're going! Helmets for infants are

much deeper at the rear to protect the back of the head better.

You'll sometimes see riders doing stunts – on jump bikes or BMXes – wearing hard-shell helmets that look

"Helmets are made from inexpensive materials. A more expensive helmet won't necessarily offer better protection"

more like skateboarding or climbing helmets. These are tough but less well ventilated. Teenagers like them, however.

Also hotter but offering more protection – most especially to the chin and face – are full-face helmets. These look like motorcycle helmets, although they're much lighter and more fragile. They're worn almost exclusively by downhill mountain bikers, who need protection much more than they need ventilation.

DOUBLE STANDARDS?

Most cycle helmets on sale today are not as tough as those on sale in the early 1990s. Then most conformed to the Snell B90 standard. Apart from the later and slightly tougher Snell B95 standard, it was – and still is – the most stringent test for cycle helmets. Each helmet is impacted more times and with more energy, on a wider variety of anvil shapes than it would be in any other helmet standard. So a helmet has to stand up to tougher blows to pass.

What's more, repeat tests are done on helmets taken from shop shelves.

The certificates you will usually see on helmets are EN 1078 (for the European market), CPSC (for the US market) and AS/NZ 2063: 1996 (for the Australian/New Zealand market). None of these is as thorough a test as Snell – according to UK helmet testing laboratory Head Protection Evaluations. The British Medical Association also favours Snell certification over the other standards.

Helmets sold in the EU have to pass EN 1078, a European-wide standard that supplanted Britain's own (and slightly better) BS 6863 in 1997. They may also pass some of the other standards.

Since there is no obligation to wear a cycle helmet at all, you don't have to wear a helmet approved to EN 1078 – or any other standard. However, if there are helmets that offer measurably better protection while also providing good weight, ventilation, comfort, and value for money, clearly they're a better buy. For that reason, I would recommend Snell B90 or B95 certified helmets – see www.smf.org.

It's a bit more complicated than that though, because helmet manufacturers often produce different models of helmet – with the same name but meeting different standards – for different markets around the world. While there are quite a few full-face helmets that meet Snell standards, only a handful of 'normal' helmets that are readily available

in the UK do so. They are all from Specialized and all carry the EN 1078 sticker here, but they're identical to the US versions: the AirForce, Aurora, Instinct, Skillet and Small Fry. At £20 and up, prices are not higher than rival helmets. See www.specialized.com for more information.

While we'd recommend these first, that isn't to say that helmets by Giro, Met, Bell and others are no better than bargain basement helmets that are also certified to EN 1708. Design, fit, ventilation, style, value and weight are all valid criteria for choosing between the rest.

DO I HAVE TO WEAR ONE?

In short: no. Compulsory cycle helmet laws does exist in some form in a number of countries, including Australia, New Zealand, parts of the United States (notably California), Canada, Spain and Sweden. Attempts have been made to pass such laws in the UK – most recently in 2004 – but have failed.

Intuitively, compulsory helmet wearing sounds like it would be a step forward in cycle safety. Insurance companies seem to think so: they have callously attempted to reduce payments to cyclists who have been hit and injured by drivers while they were not wearing helmets. Presumably these unhelmeted cyclists were 'asking for it, your honour…' And there are lots of anecdotes from cyclists along the lines of 'my bicycle helmet saved my life'. Of course, we don't know if it

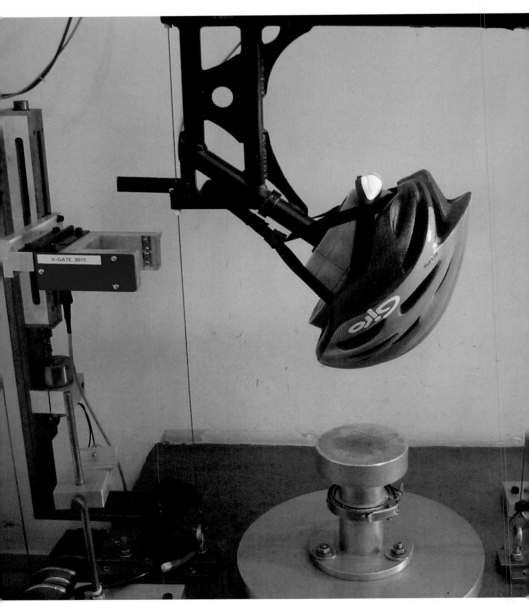

To be certified, helmets are tested by being smashed into a variety of anvil shapes. Different standards use different testing regimes. Snell's standards are the most stringent. Photo: HPE/Brian Walker

did or not. The number of fatal head injuries to unhelmeted cyclists would suggest not.

Either way, the anecdotes don't reflect the big picture. Statistics do. That's why there's resistance to compulsory helmet wearing among UK cyclists. Not because of a libertarian dream to feel the wind in one's hair, but because the safety data, unlike the anecdotes, doesn't support mandatory usage. (Note well that word 'mandatory'. Hardly anyone is against helmet usage. It's the legal obligation that's the sticking point.)

Cycling is not a dangerously risky activity. Per mile, you're more likely to be killed while walking than cycling. Six times more pedestrians – and 18 times more car drivers – suffer lethal head injuries than cyclists. Yet no one is advocating pedestrian or car helmets, apart from those for Formula One racing drivers. The British Medical Association has calculated (as 'life years gained' versus 'life years lost') that the benefits to health from regular cycling outweigh all the risks by a factor of 20 to 1.

It is curious that the countries with the highest levels of cycling and the lowest levels of risk to cyclists are those where cycle helmet wearing is negligible – for example, the Netherlands and Denmark.

In countries where helmets have been made compulsory, cycling levels have fallen – by an average of 30% in Australia – without a matching fall in head injuries. And Australia now trails the United States as the most obese country on the planet.

There is strong evidence that helmets help prevent scalp injuries. Beyond that, the evidence is hotly contested. It seems likely – to me, at least – that helmets lessen the effect of impact injuries in those circumstances for which they're designed. Yet, at the same time, it's quite possible that they increase the incidence of rotational brain injuries and neck injuries.

So should you wear one? Only you can answer. At the end of the day cycling is good for you, and is not, in the grand scheme of things, dangerous. If wearing a helmet makes you feel safer and thus more likely

"Cycling is not a dangerous activity. Per mile, you're more likely to be killed while walking than cycling"

to cycle, it's worth wearing one. If having to wear a helmet makes it less likely you would cycle, then don't wear one – or just wear one in those circumstances that you think it necessary or useful. 'Sometimes' is just as valid a response as 'always' or 'never'; I always wear a helmet for mountain biking but don't wear one all the time on my other bikes.

For lots more information on this topic, have a look at the Bicycle Helmet Research Foundation website: cyclehelmets.org.

Luggage

CARRYING THINGS BY BICYCLE
is easier than it is on foot. That's
because you've always got a great set
of luggage wheels: the bike's. Whether
it's a picnic, a school bag or the weekly
grocery shop, you can move it quickly
and easily by bike.

As your hands are on the handlebars,
carrying anything in them is not an
option. Nor is hanging bags from
the ends of the handlebars, which
compromises the steering and creates
the risk of a bag catching in the front
wheel. Your options are: on your back;
on the bike; or in a trailer. That's the
order for weight and volume, too. Light
loads can easily go on your back, but
big things really have to go in a trailer.
In between, there's the bike.

ON YOUR BACK

Carrying a load on your back can make
it really ache. On a bike you're bent
over rather than upright, which isn't
a good posture for carrying loads. It
means your hands and backside have
more weight bearing down on them.
It also makes you hotter, so you sweat
more. Most of the time you're better off
letting the bike be the beast of burden.

There are exceptions. If you're riding
a mountain bike over rough terrain,
any dead weight on the bike will
deaden the handling. If the weight
moves with you on your back then you
can still move the bike around nimbly
beneath you. A hydration pack – like a

rucksack but also containing a water
bladder with a long tube – does away
with the need for water bottles on the
bike too. As such, it's standard kit for
technically demanding off-road rides.
Some hydration packs accommodate
only the water bladder and enough
room for a few tools; others are big
enough (20 litres of luggage space) for
several days away, if you pack light.

Features to look for in hydration
packs include waist and sternum
straps to keep the load close to
your body, and – if it's a bigger bag
– compression straps to cinch down
a loose load. Good brands include
CamelBak, who pioneered the idea
(www.zyro.eu.com), Hydrapak (www.
ultimatepursuits.co.uk) and Dakine
(www.dakine.com). Expect to pay
from £25 upwards.

The other cyclists who carry loads
on their back are cycle couriers.
That's because they're on and off their
bikes all day, making lots of stops.
The load goes with them as soon as
they dismount. That get-off-and-go
simplicity can make a backpack just as
useful for short trips by any cyclist, so
long as the load isn't too heavy.

Courier-style shoulder bags look
cool. However, when you lean forward
on a bike the bag can creep round until
it's hanging off one side and banging
your knee. The more you lean forward
– for instance, on drop handlebars
– the more of a problem that this is.

The other disadvantage is that one shoulder bears the bulk of the weight. Still, if this is your thing, Crumpler (www.crumpler.co.uk) and Ortlieb (www.ortlieb.com) make some of the best on the market.

A backpack-style bag is more comfortable and more secure – particularly if, like a mountain biker's hydration pack, it's got waist and sternum straps. If you're using a walker's rucksack, use a small one – a daypack rather than a towering backpack, which will unbalance you. Better still is a compact waterproof one like Ortlieb's Velocity (£55), whose 20-litre capacity will carry as much as you'd want to put on your back.

ON THE BIKE

The further you plan to travel and the more you've got to carry, the more it makes sense to put at least some of the load on the bike.

All bikes can carry some luggage. Those that can carry panniers give the most options and the biggest capacity. You may see expedition cyclists with bags all over their bikes – two rear panniers, two front ones, a bar bag, a rack pack and a seat pack. For shorter trips, all you really need is two panniers on a rear carrier rack.

To fit that carrier rack, you want a bike with eyelets by the rear dropouts and on the seatstays. The bottom eyelets are the most important, as they bear most of the load. You can use P-clips to substitute for the top set. (Ask your bike shop or visit www.ctcshop.

A backpack is fine for carrying light loads a short distance. Otherwise, let the bike take the strain. Photo: Cycling Images

com, which stocks Tortec P-clips for £2.99 a pair.) Or you can use a seat clamp with integral rack eyelets, such as the one by M:Part (£5.99). If you also want to fit a front rack, it needs eyelets at the dropouts and low-rider mounts on the fork legs – most bikes don't have these.

The rear rack itself needs to be fairly sturdy. Get one that attaches at four points rather than three, as it won't flex from side to side as much under load. Racks made from steel tubing are the stiffest and strongest. Tubus (www.tubus.com) make the best, although at £70 or so they're not cheap. Racks from thick aluminium rod are fine for most purposes. Blackburn build some good ones, such as the EX1+ (£30, www.ultimatepursuits.co.uk). The Revolution Adventure Pannier Rack Expedition is a fairly faithful copy for just £13 (www.edinburghbicycle.com).

BAGS FOR THE BIKE

Panniers are available in two rough sizes: rear panniers, which have a volume of 20-25 litres each, and front panniers – sometimes called 'universal' panniers – which have that sort of volume per pair. Rear panniers are sometimes left or right specific: the front edge of the pannier tapers sharply to avoid the rider's heel when pedalling. Being smaller, front/universal panniers don't have this problem if you fit them to a rear rack. Why would you want to? You might not need the space of big rear panniers.

The golden rule of pannier packing is: your luggage will expand or contract to fit the space available. If you use big panniers, you'll fill them. If you use small panniers, you'll fill them too – but with a lighter load that's easier to carry.

For a long weekend away in the UK, around 25 litres of luggage space per person should be plenty, assuming you're staying at B&Bs, hotels or youth hostels. By way of comparison, a typical medium-sized suitcase holds 60 litres, so two rear panniers should hold all your holiday gear for a fortnight… For a more stable load, pack your heavier items at the bottom of the bags.

For shorter journeys, such as day trips, commuting or going to school, one or two universal panniers should be plenty. The problem will come if you need to transport A4 files or papers. They'll get dog-eared in a small pannier. One solution is to use a bigger pannier. A more elegant one is to use an office pannier. This is a briefcase-style bag that fits onto the rack at an angle to provide enough heel clearance, while easily accommodating files, papers – even a laptop computer, if you add a padded insert. Ortlieb's Office Bag (£70) is the best, being well made and completely waterproof. Other good ones are made by Carradice (www.carradice.co.uk) and Altura (www.zyro.eu.com).

The same brands, along with Agu (www.ulimatepursuits.co.uk) and VauDe (www.vaude.com) make excellent normal panniers. Expect to pay £50-£70 for a front/universal pair and £70-£90 for a rear set. My favourites are Carradice Super C and Ortlieb Roller Classic bags.

You can get cheap nylon panniers for much less than this – under £30 for a rear set is likely. These are fine to begin with but they won't be as tough and won't be waterproof, so use plastic bags inside to keep things dry. Some lack the stiff backplate of quality panniers too, so you may need to pack carefully or use a pannier rack with a dogleg rear strut to keep the rear corner of the pannier out of the wheel.

Not all bikes can be fitted with a rear rack, and there are others you

Two rear panniers will carry almost as much luggage as a typical suitcase. If that's not enough, you can use front panniers as well or strap a load across the top of the rear rack. Photo: Cycling Images

might not want to fit with a rear rack. There's still the saddle or seat post to attach bags to. Smaller bags, often referred to as seat-packs rather than saddlebags, clip to a bracket fixed to the saddle rails and are stabilised by a strap wrapped around the seat post. With small capacities (usually around one litre or so), they're best for tools, a spare inner tube and perhaps an energy bar or two. Topeak's Expando Wedge Bags (from £10, www.extrauk. co.uk) are good.

Saddlebags also attach to the saddle rails or to a bracket on the seat post but are much bigger. Carradice's Super C Saddlebag (£52) has a capacity of 23 litres – enough for all your weekend luggage. There are lots of others too. See www.carradice.co.uk.

TRAILERS

A child trailer (see Chapter 2) will carry a week's groceries for a family. It's easier than using panniers as you can just lift the bags from the trolley to the trailer, instead of decanting the shopping bit by bit.

If you want a dedicated luggage trailer – either for carrying touring loads like the family tent behind a tandem, or for bulky loads – the Carry Freedom Y-Frame is great (from £180, www.carryfreedom.com). For really heavy haulage, you need a load-carrying bike or trike (see Chapter 2).

Lighting

THE LAW SAYS THAT if you ride a bicycle on a UK public road between dusk and dawn you must use a white front light and a red rear light. You must also have a red rear reflector and amber pedal reflectors.

The lights must be marked as conforming to BS6102/3 or an equivalent EC standard. That's assuming they emit (or can emit) a steady light, which most lights do. Lights that can only flash are now allowed if they're sufficiently bright ('four candela'), despite the fact that flashing lights are not yet covered by BS6102/3...

The regulations are a bit of a mess as it stands. A rechargeable set-up that lights up the night with 80 Watts of brilliance? Illegal. A dynamo lighting set that goes out completely when you stop? Legal. That little blinky LED? Might be legal, might not.

The good news is that the police sensibly turn a blind eye: if you've got reasonable lights and they're the right colour, then they're content. The bad news is that a lawyer might take a different view. If you were in an accident at night and were using 'unapproved' lights, the lawyer could try to make a case for contributory negligence.

You can legally use unapproved lights in addition to approved ones. You just need one front and one rear light that is legal.

Dynamo lights provide fit-and-forget lighting that's always available and won't run down. Photo: Cycling Images

DISPOSABLE BATTERY LIGHTS

In Britain, disposable-battery lights with filament bulbs are still a popular form of illumination. They're okay if you're riding across town occasionally. If you're riding often you'll exhaust a set of alkaline batteries every week. Few such lights have burn times longer than 10 hours, even on alkalines; most are lower. So while initial purchase prices are low, running costs are high.

It's possible to substitute rechargeable batteries, even though these usually have a lower voltage

(1.2V versus 1.5V). The Cateye HL500 (£15, www.zyro.eu.com) converts well to rechargeables and is a decent lamp in any case. Illumination with clip-on battery lamps is fine under streetlights. You can just about get by on unlit lanes if you cycle with care and at moderate speed – or add a second front light.

LEDs are replacing filament bulbs in all areas of cycle lighting. Burn times are much longer and so is the bulb life. While LEDs do red light best – to the extent that there's little reason to use anything else for your rear light, whether it's dynamo or battery powered – white LEDs have lately become much better. They're not as good as red rear lights, because the light has to be filtered through a phosphor coating to turn it white, which means that more power is required for an equivalent brightness. Yet compared to filament bulb lamps, they're still super efficient lights. Some are even BS-approved, such as Cateye's EL300/AU100BS lighting set (which costs £45).

You can substitute rechargeable batteries in LED lights, although the under-volting of these more efficient lights can cause a slight dimming. Red rear LED lights consume so little power and last so long – up to 100 hours or more on a set of alkaline batteries – that using rechargeables isn't such an economic or environmental necessity. Nevertheless, it's better to use larger batteries for longer burn times – that

is, lamps that use AA size batteries rather than AAA.

DYNAMO LIGHTS
Dynamo lights are the norm in European countries where utility cycling is popular, such as Germany and Holland. They provide fit-and-forget lighting that's always available and won't run down at the cost of a little drag. It really is a little, too – considerably less than 1mph off your speed with a bottle dynamo, and way below 0.5mph with a more efficient hub dynamo.

Almost all dynamos are 6 Volt systems, powering a 2.4 Watt front lamp and 0.6 Watt rear. If you run a battery-powered rear light (LED, of course) then you can fit a 3 Watt bulb up front for extra brightness. Lacking raw power, a lot of work has gone into making dynamo lamps make the best use of the power they have, and even a 2.4W front lamp will provide enough light for unlit lanes.

'Bottle' dynamos that run off the sidewall of the tyre are the cheapest and most common. They work better if the tyre has a file-pattern dynamo track on the sidewell. Some slip badly in the rain, which means you lose power – and light! – while the better ones (Axa, Lightspin, Busch und Müller, Nordlicht) cope with most conditions short of snow, sleet and mud. Expect to pay from £15 for the lamp(s) and twice that for the dynamo.

Hub dynamos, which do the power-generation inside a dedicated hub, outperform sidewall dynamos. The drag is much lower and they don't slip. The disadvantages are that they're more expensive and they have to be built into a wheel. Expect to pay from about £60 for a wheel using Shimano's most basic Nexus hub dynamo (from www.ctcshop.com for example) or from around £160 for a wheel built using the most efficient, best dynamo there is – the Schmidt 28 Dynohub (see www.sjscycles.co.uk).

> "Cheaper systems use basic lamps and sealed lead acid batteries, like car batteries. These are heavy but okay"

Better dynamo lamps incorporate a stand-light, which comes on when you stop. This is a secondary LED in the lamp, or just the main LED if it's an LED lamp. Batteries aren't needed: the dynamo charges a capacitor, which powers the LED. It's not bright enough to see by, but it's enough to be seen by.

There's an interesting new generator lighting system from Danish company Reelight (www.reelight.com) that works by magnetic induction. The LED lamps mount to the wheel axles and you fit magnets to the spokes. As the wheels revolve, the magnets pass the sensors in the lamps and the tiny pulse of energy this produces is enough to light them. They're ideal for town use, being legal and long-lasting.

RECHARGEABLE LIGHTS

Rechargeable 'system' lights with high-quality battery packs offer awesome, car-headlight style illumination – for a price (£100-plus). The more tightly defined your riding pattern on a particular bike (e.g. a regular commute or a twice-weekly ride), and the faster you wish to ride, the more you can make a case for a rechargeable system over a dynamo set-up. And if you want to go off-road at all, it's a no brainer: get a rechargeable system. As a rule of thumb, you need at least 10W of lighting off-road.

Cheaper systems use basic lamps and sealed lead acid batteries, like car batteries. These are heavy for the power output, but otherwise okay. The brightest lights use Lithium-ion (Li-ion) batteries and High Intensity Discharge (HID) lamps, which you'll know better as arc lamps. Nickel-metal-hydride (NiMH) batteries still offer good performance, and halogen bulbs are still effective, particularly when a tightly focused spotlight is combined with a wider-angled floodlight. Both types could soon be history: the future, as with all cycle lighting, belongs to LEDs. Have a look at the expensive but lovely products from Exposure (www.amba-marketing.com) and Dinotte (www.on-one-shop.co.uk).

The batteries the lamps require fit in the bike's bottle cage or are strapped to the frame. Burn times, even with large batteries, aren't great because of the power that high-wattage lamps

Night-riding off-road requires powerful rechargeable lights. As a rule of thumb, a 10 Watt halogen lamp or its equivalent is the bare minimum. Photo: Seb Rogers

draw. Two to four hours is about average, which is fine for an evening's mountain biking. LED lamps draw less power and result in smaller batteries and longer burn times.

You can expect to recharge the battery up to 500 times before it dies, probably less. It helps to use a smart charger, which stops pumping power into the battery and cooking it when it's full. If you do use a normal, slow charger, use a wall-socket timer.

BIKE LIGHT SECURITY

Lots of battery and rechargeable lights clip on and off easily, with just a small screw-on bracket staying on the bike. This is handy for switching one set of lights between bikes (especially if you buy extra brackets). It also neatly avoids the problem of theft. The downside is that you have to fuss with your bike for a few moments before and after riding and then carry the lamps around – with the risk that they will switch themselves on in the bottom of your bag.

What's more, quick releases can release at the wrong moment: when you hit a pothole your light can be ejected onto the tarmac with a crash. Lights that bolt in place – dynamo lights and rack-fitting lights – stay put. Theft is rare, as it's too much hassle; few thieves carry an 8mm spanner. Vandalism is a risk, however.

Security

MORE THAN 100,000 bicycles are stolen every year in the UK. Hardly any are recovered. If you cannot park your bike behind a locked door whenever you leave it, you need a bike lock.

Some locks are truly awful. I've seen a cable lock cut with a pair of scissors. U-locks with cylindrical keys have famously been picked with a Biro pen top, forcing a mass recall by a manufacturer. And I once sawed through a cheap U-lock with a junior hacksaw... While any lock is better than no lock, it helps to be aware of the level of protection you're buying.

In the UK locks can be – but aren't required to be – tested by Sold Secure, a not-for-profit company administered by the Master Locksmiths Association. They rate locks Bronze, Silver or Gold in ascending order of security. The locks should hold out for one, three and five minutes respectively against progressively more determined and tooled-up attacks.

> "Always use your lock. Without a lock, anyone can steal your bike. If it's locked, only lock-breakers can attempt it"

It's not a bad guide to quality if you take the times listed with a pinch of salt. Even without power tools, a thief with big bolt croppers or a stubby bottle jack can break open Gold-rated locks in under a minute. That doesn't mean locks are useless. Most will stop an opportunist thief and good ones can make it hard enough work for a professional thief that he'll look for easier pickings.

HOW TO USE A LOCK

The key, if you'll excuse the pun, is to use the lock wisely. First of all: always use it. If you turn your back on your bike even for a few seconds, lock it. Lots of cyclists have just nipped into a shop only to find their bike gone on coming out. Without a lock, anyone can steal your bike. If it's locked, only lock-breakers can attempt it.

Thieves don't like an audience, so lock your bike in a public place rather than down an alleyway. Lock it through the frame to a solid, immovable object such as a bike stand or iron railings. Make sure the object is a closed loop, so the thief can't lift the bike over the top, and don't use anything flimsy or the thief will cut that instead of the lock.

If you're using a U-lock, it's better to lock the bike low down around the bottom bracket or seat-tube rather than over the top-tube, where the thief can get at it easily. Fill the shackle of the lock with as much bike and street furniture as will fit, leaving as little daylight in the lock as possible. It makes the lock harder to attack. A

Whichever type of lock you're using, it's important to make sure you use it properly. It's no use spending good money on a strong lock and then just securing a front wheel or this will happen... Photo: istock

shorter, narrower lock is harder to attack than a big one, though it is more awkward to attach in some situations.

If you're using a flexible lock such as a cable or a chain, wrap it in such a way to keep it fairly taught. Again, this makes it harder for the thief to attack it with cable cutters or bolt croppers.

If you've got a Gold-standard lock with a proper (not cylindrical) key from the likes of Abus, Squire, Kryptonite or Trelock, the lock itself will be fairly pick-proof and drill-proof. Nevertheless, if you can make the locking mechanism harder to get at it's worth doing so.

Don't forget to keep a spare key somewhere safe. All locks can be broken but that doesn't mean that lock-breaking is easy.

You'll need to oil the lock occasionally to prevent it seizing. Squirt a bit of oil into any holes and work it in by repeatedly opening and closing the lock. If your lock freezes solid in winter, pour hot water over it and oil it afterwards.

TYPES OF LOCK

Locks range from thin wires to thick chains that could be used to moor trawlers. The more security you want and the more you pay, the heavier the lock will be... and therefore, the harder it will be to haul around.

Thin cable locks are more properly

Lock your bike when you leave it. It will stop casual thieves and should slow down pros. Photos: Cycling Images/Carlton Reid

called immobilisers, not locks. The lightest use retractable 2mm wire cables and a combination lock in a plastic body the size of a mobile phone. They're fine for café and loo stops where you're away from your bike for moments. They won't stop a thief, or anyone armed with cable cutters. The Abus Combiflex 202 (£15, www.zyro.eu.com) is a good example of this type.

Thicker cable locks look like they offer lots more security than this. They don't. A 7mm cable is harder to cut than a 2mm cable, but not that much, and sometimes the thickness is extra plastic. As a lock to foil kids and to get your children into the security habit, you could do worse. Just don't expect great protection.

U-locks (or D-locks) are probably the best compromise between portability and security for town cyclists, as they're easily carried in brackets fixed to the frame. Opportunists won't even attempt to attack them, so any Gold or even Silver standard U-lock is usually sufficient. For high-risk areas or more expensive bikes, consider a U-lock with a narrower and/or shorter shackle, such as the Abus Granit Futura 64 120/230 (£65) or the Kryptonite Fahgettaboudit U-lock (£75, www.kryptonitelock.com).

If you don't mind the weight, a motorcycle-style security chain offers the best protection. They're also great for home use, with a ground or wall anchor. Many of these can still be bolt-cropped. Top pick, as it's practically uncroppable: the Almax Immobiliser Series III with Squire padlock (from £90, www.almax-security-chains.co.uk). Get a long one and loop it through three or four bikes.

A useful Continental-style lock you don't see so often in Britain is the frame- or wheel-lock, also known as a nurse's lock. It fits permanently to a bike's seat-stays. It works by means of a locking bar going between the

"If your bike does get stolen, report the theft to the police. It's a requirement of insurance policies"

spokes of the back wheel, preventing anyone riding off on the bike. Security isn't super high, but it's always there so you're never without a lock. One that's widely available in the UK is the Abus 49 Uni Frame Ringo (£16).

BITS AND PIECES

Even if your bike is securely locked, thieves may half-inch parts from it. Anything with a quick release skewer can be removed in moments by anyone. A bike that's locked up in town needs more protection than this.

A quick-and-dirty solution is to bind the quick release levers to the frame using plumber's metal hose clamps. A better option is to use Allen bolts instead of quick releases. Better still is a set of security skewers. These have specific, individual bolt heads that

require a dedicated tool to undo. The Pinhead Four Pack (£50, www.2pure.co.uk) will keep your wheels, seat and fork safe.

STOLEN PROPERTY

If, despite your precautions, your bike does get stolen, report the theft to the police. It's unlikely anything will happen, but it's a requirement of insurance policies that you do this. Your bikes are insured, right?

Some household policies include bike insurance. Check the small print. Often the maximum bike value is £300 or so, or else it doesn't cover the bike when you're out and about. Cycle-specific insurance does exist – try CTC Cyclecover (www.cyclecover.co.uk).

Some locks come with a several hundred pound guarantee should your bike be stolen. Again, check the small print. The requirement may be that you send the broken lock. Thieves seldom leave broken locks.

AND FINALLY...

Theft does happen but it isn't inevitable. Most bikes that are stolen are either locked with cheap and nasty locks or else not locked at all. With a reasonable lock and a sensible attitude you're almost certain to keep your bike safe and secure.

Impress this on your children, especially teenagers whose mountain bikes are prime targets. Give your teen a lock and make sure – if the bike will be unattended at any point – that he or she doesn't leave home without it.

Useful extras

To carry three or four bikes, you're better off with a tow-bar mounted rack or a roof rack. Photo: Cycling Images

A PUMP AND a puncture outfit are essential on any ride that goes further than you'd want to walk back from. We'll look at those in Chapter 9. So what about other accessories?

Bells are required to be sold with all new bicycles. It's up to you whether you keep the bell on the bike. Bells can be useful for alerting pedestrians or horse-riders to your presence, particularly on shared-use paths. They're less useful in traffic. Car drivers can't hear them. If a pedestrian suddenly steps into the road in front

of you it's safer to shout a warning and either brake or take evasive action than it is to ring your bell.

Mirrors are useful for keeping an eye on children travelling behind you in a seat, trailer or trailer cycle. You can keep an eye on following traffic too. Don't depend on the mirror before any manoeuvres. Looking behind gives you a better view and lets motorists know you're about to do something.

MUDGUARDS

Getting rained on is bad enough but the constant spray of cold, dirty water from your wheels on wet days is worse. Unless you ride in full cycling kit, you'll want mudguards.

You can fit some sort of mudguard to any bike. Mountain bikes can be fitted with partial guards. They attach at the rear to the seat-post and at the front either to the down-tube or under the fork crown. They won't keep you completely dry but they will keep the worst off. The long-established Mr Crud Raceguard (£14, www.ultimatepursuits.co.uk) and Crudcatcher (£8) are still among the best, while Topeak (www.extrauk.co.uk) and SKS (www.chickencycles.co.uk) make decent rival 'guards.

Road bikes and hybrids that don't have sufficient clearance for full mudguards can be fitted with partial 'guards. They look like sawn-in-half 'guards and fit to the fork and seat-stays. SKS pioneered the idea with their Race Blades (£35), and there are cheaper copies available.

If your bike has mudguard eyelets and enough clearance to fit full mudguards – you need about 10mm of air between tyre and mudguard to let grit rattle through – then you want a set of SKS Chromoplastics or SKS Bluemels guards. They come in all kinds of widths and for 700C or 26in wheels. At £18-£25, prices aren't much higher than rivals. Quality is better and so is safety: the front stays are designed to snap off and release if anything gets jammed under the 'guard, which could prevent a nasty accident. You can fit 26in-wheel 'guards to a child's bike with 24in wheels. There's enough flexibility for the tighter radius bend and they don't wrap so far that they hit the ground.

CAR RACKS

Strictly speaking, a bike carrier is a car accessory, but then the car itself is a cycle accessory, inasmuch as it gets bikes and cyclists to the start of rides. That might be a mountain bike ride, a ride on a Sustrans trail, or the family holiday where the bikes go too.

Two adults can use a cheap, strap-on bike carrier to transport the bikes, or else put the partially disassembled bikes in the back of the car. That's not an option for the average family of four. At best there will be room for one bike (wheels off) in the boot, maybe two if it's a big car, because the seats will be occupied.

While some have room for three, strap-on racks aren't really sturdy enough for more than two bikes. That leaves tow-bar mounted racks and roof racks, which will each carry up to four bikes.

Tow-bar racks are much easier to get the bikes on and off, but make the vehicle longer and harder to park. The bikes get dirtier too. Wheel-support tow-bar racks hold the bikes better than those that hook the top-tubes on support arms. Many wheel-support racks will pivot out of the way to give access to the boot. You'll obviously need a tow-bar, and you'll likely need a lighting board as it's illegal to obscure your rear numberplate and lights.

Roof-racks put the bikes out of the way, so long as you're strong and tall enough to get them up there. The vehicle will be much higher, so low-bridges, branches and car-park barriers will be impassable. Fuel efficiency drops significantly whenever you carry bikes outside the car, and roof-mounted bikes are the least efficient. You'll need to buy roof bars and then as many bike supports as required. You can fit four on most cars, by having the bikes face alternate directions, or two plus a roofbox.

Strap on racks cost £50-£100. For tow-bar or roof-racks expect to spend £200-300, maybe more once you factor in all the bits. Two reliable brands are Thule (www.thule.co.uk) and Pendle (www.pendle-bike.co.uk).

Don't forget to lock your bikes onto the rack when you leave the vehicle.

Photo: Cycling Images

THE PERCEIVED RISK from the traffic on today's roads puts a lot of people off cycling on them, especially families. Here's the thing: it might feel less safe today but it isn't. You're actually safer now than you would have been in those halcyon days of 1950, when there were far fewer drivers. (There were more cycling fatalities, per billion kilometres cycled, in 1950 than there were in 2006.) It's more pleasant to ride on country lanes and back-roads than busy trunk roads, and you can often plot your trips so you can do just that. However, dense traffic tends to be slower traffic, and heavily-used urban roads can be quite safe for cycling so long as you ride sensibly and assertively.

Assertiveness is key. You don't have to get out of the way for the traffic: *you are the traffic.* That's not cyclists' rhetoric. If you hide in the gutter and ride submissively, you are less safe than if you're out there in the traffic stream, integrating with other road users.

Riding in traffic is about dealing with people. Car drivers aren't out to get you; like you, they're out to get somewhere. So long as they see you and understand what you're doing – both things that you can help them with – there's no cause for concern. If you act like traffic, you will be treated like traffic. This can be a big leap if you're new to cycling. It's a big topic too. The guidelines here are just a primer. I recommend that you get a copy of Cyclecraft (£12, www.cyclecraft. co.uk). You may also want to get some training. See www.ctc.org. uk/cycletraining or call the Cycle Training Helpline on 0870 607 0415.

You may remember cycle training in the form of the cycling proficiency test. It's evolved since then. It's not just for children, for one thing. However, children have much less experience as road users. Before they make journeys on their own, some kind of training – with an accredited provider or with you – is vital.

Children can ride on roads accompanied by you from a much younger age than they would solo, because you're there to handle the negotiation and integration with the traffic. There will come a day when they're ready to make independent journeys, such as cycling to school. It won't be until after they're capable of walking to school alone and it might not be until they get to secondary school. But given the skills, they can do it. Cyclists are made, not born.

Cycling in traffic

BEFORE YOU RIDE with your children on trafficked roads, you need to be comfortable cycling by yourself in that environment. Not until you can take care of yourself on the road can you safely take others out with you.

The first requirement is that you're a competent cyclist. You have to be able to stop, start, steer, brake, change gear, take one hand off the handlebars to signal, and look behind while going in a straight line. If you can't, practise away from traffic, or get trained.

> "Don't feel guilty about taking the lane. You're not blocking drivers but being safe by controlling the space around you"

There are two more things you need. One is a heightened awareness of what's going on around you. A bit like a car driver on a motorway, you don't just look dead ahead. You observe what's around you, checking side roads, looking for pedestrians about to step off pavements, etc. You need to use your ears too. Sound is your first warning of following traffic, which is why it's a bad idea to cycle with an MP3 player or to talk on a mobile phone, even though it's not illegal.

The other thing you need is assertiveness. Not aggressiveness or a holier-than-thou attitude, just self-confidence. You have as much right to be on the road and to get where you want to go as anyone else. Sometimes you will have to wait for other traffic and sometimes other traffic will have to wait for you. Don't be timid: let other road users know what you're going to do and – if it's safe – do it.

POSITIONING

A big part of assertive cycling is where you ride. Make sure it's not in the gutter. The road surface is poor there, because of drains, potholes, and detritus like broken glass that's been swept to the road edge by car tyres.

Worse than that is the fact that you're outside of the traffic stream, the main current in which motor traffic moves. It makes you less visible to all other road users – drivers behind you, drivers at junctions ahead, pedestrians – because they will be focusing on where they expect traffic to be, which is in that zone. If you're in someone's peripheral vision, you're easy to overlook. If you're right there where they're looking, you stand out.

At first it feels vulnerable to be further out from the kerb and you might worry that you are 'in the way of drivers'. In fact, rear end collisions are extremely rare for cyclists. Hugging the kerb is riskier because it invites motorists to squeeze past. If you're riding further out it obliges traffic to overtake you as if you were a car (or perhaps a tractor), which is just what the Highway Code requires of drivers – see Rule 163. As a rule of thumb, the distance you are from the kerb is the distance that overtaking drivers will give you.

Cycle trainers describe being in the traffic stream as 'taking the lane'. When you're cycling briskly in town, there's little conflict because a car's speed won't be very different from yours. Sometimes you'll be cycling much slower than the traffic. That's true for children or for less confident cyclists. Or perhaps it's uphill or a fast road. In those cases there's a secondary position you can adopt, which is just to the left of the traffic stream. Even then, keep out of the gutter. Don't go within 50cm of the kerb: 75cm to a metre is better.

Don't feel guilty about taking the lane. You're not blocking drivers but keeping yourself safe by controlling the space around you – for example, preventing drivers from overtaking where it is unsafe to do so. The extra space is a buffer zone too. It provides you with extra room to manoeuvre.

MANOEUVRES

Before you change your position on the road, it's essential to look behind to check for following traffic. Simply looking alerts drivers that you're about to do something. Then signal clearly and boldly – arm straight out. Don't start to move out immediately. You are signalling your intention. By making

If you ride too close to the kerb, it invites drivers to squeeze past without giving you enough room. Photo: Cycling Images

eye contact with the driver behind, you can assess whether it's safe to start moving. Most drivers will give way; a few will accelerate.

If it's safe, start to move out and keep your arm out until you've gone as far out as you're going. You want to be moving out at a shallow angle rather than suddenly, so start your manoeuvre early.

If you're overtaking a parked car, be sure to leave at least a door's width between you and it in case a door gets opened in your path. If you're turning right, you're aiming for a position just left of the white line in the middle of your road. You will need to stop and wait here if there's no gap in the oncoming traffic, or no gap in either direction if you're turning right from a side road. When you make the turn, don't cut the corner. Go right like a chess knight, not a bishop.

Turning left is easier. You still need to signal, but need not do so as early. Take the turn fairly wide. If you take it tight, you may get forced into the kerb by following traffic that's also turning left and decides to overtake you here. Take that lane!

If you're going straight on at a junction, such as a crossroads, once again, take the lane. Otherwise left-turning traffic may cut across in front of you.

When you're approaching junctions, it's common to find long rows of stationary traffic. It's permissible to overtake such traffic, and at traffic lights where there are advanced stop lines for cyclists it is often preferable to do so. Normal overtaking procedure is to pass on the right, moving back in to take the lane when you're done.

What about passing on the inside, which is rather ominously known as 'undertaking'? With care, a cyclist can pass stationary traffic like this. As before, the aim is to pass and then move back in to take the lane. Sitting in the gutter next to traffic is not good. If the car next to you goes left up ahead and you go straight on, you'll have to make an emergency stop or crash. This is a matter of life and death with long vehicles. NEVER undertake a long vehicle like an articulated lorry or a bus. If it sets off and goes left, you could die, squashed against railings or crushed under the rear wheels, which always corner in a tighter arc than the front wheels.

Even if you are where you should be on the road, and you're alert, some situations require evasive action. Maybe a motorist pulls out right in front of you. You've got three choices: brake, swerve, or accelerate. Circumstances will dictate which is best.

An emergency stop is harder on a bike than in a car. Your brakes aren't as good, and if you lock the wheels the resulting skid could cause you to crash. Practise stopping suddenly away from traffic to see what it's like. Use both brakes and slide back off the saddle to counter the fact that your bodyweight will be thrown forward as you decelerate.

Swerving is fastest if you start to turn your bars (but not your body) the opposite way you want to go, then turn them back and 'fall into' the turn. This isn't something you can rationalise in a split second so don't try. Set up a few markers away from traffic and practise slaloming between them. You should soon be able to thread the bike past while your body carries on in more or less a straight line. Alternatively, take up mountain biking. It will do wonders for your bike handling.

Accelerating is only an option if you can read the traffic well enough to know what happens next. It gets you out of trouble before it arrives.

Photo: Martin Breschinski, courtesy of Transport for London

6.2 Cycling in traffic

KNOW YOUR ROAD FEATURES

Basic manoeuvres are fine for travelling along a smooth tarmac road with a straightforward layout. Sadly the road environment isn't that simple. Today's highway engineers have a suite of design features to choose from that's as varied as a spoiled kid's Scalextric track box. Chicanes and awkward crossroads are just the start.

Roundabouts cause some cyclists problems. It doesn't help that the Highway Code gives pretty risky advice on the subject. Keeping to the left doesn't make you safer: it makes you more likely to be run over by a driver who hasn't seen you. When you approach a roundabout, take your lane – even if you're going left – as it will stop you getting squeezed by traffic doing the same. If you're going straight on or right, it's generally safer to head for the middle of the roundabout and then look, signal and peel off at the appropriate exit. If you're riding around the edge, you have to deal with traffic coming onto and off the roundabout, precisely where you're riding. And as you're on the periphery, the drivers may not have seen you. In the middle, traffic can see you and can only pass you on your left.

Traffic calming is a two-edged sword for cyclists. Slower traffic is good. Some of the calming measures are not. Those that narrow the width of the road increase the risk that traffic will overtake where there is no room to do so. Traffic islands in the middle of the road are the most common, but sometimes the road narrows on both sides with a give-way marking on one of the carriageways. Sometimes there are chicanes. Your response is the same and you can probably guess it: take the lane. If there is no room for traffic to pass safely it's best if it doesn't pass at all.

> "Level crossings and tram tracks are very slippery when they're wet. Always cross them at a perpendicular angle"

Speed humps or speed cushions also require care. The bumps can be quite abrupt. Stand up on the pedals slightly so your weight is off the saddle and keep your elbows and knees slightly bent. You can then use your body to absorb the bump. Make sure you approach any hump or cushion square on, and be alert for following traffic racing between humps and then braking or swerving left or right to go over the hump(s) in a different way.

Rising out of the saddle can work for potholes. It depends on the size of the hole and the bike you're riding. Large wheels with fat tyres will shrug off a hole that might stop a small-wheeled bike dead. If it looks rideable, rise up out of the saddle and let the bike roll through it. Your feet must have a secure grip on the pedals for this to work, or else they might be jolted off. Clipless pedals or pedals with toe-straps are ideal. Rain-wet flat pedals are not. If you're not sure of your footing, stay seated and take the hit. Of course, the best solution is not to run into the pothole at all. If you're riding sufficiently far out from the kerb, you have room for manoeuvre. Use it.

Roads can be very slippery after rain. If you have to ride over drain covers or shiny tarmac sealing lines, make sure you're going in a straight line and don't brake on top of them. A road that's been dry for a while and suddenly gets wet seems to bring dried oil spillages to the surface, so take care at junctions and roundabouts. Black ice is worse and can form anywhere. It tends to reform in the same place, so make a mental note if you hit any.

Level crossings and tram tracks deserve special mention. They're very slippery when they're wet and it's possible to slip on them even when they're not, especially if you cross them at an acute angle. Always cross level crossings and tram tracks as near to perpendicular as possible. Do the same for cattle grids, keeping an eye out for any longitudinal gaps.

Cycle lanes marked on roads and separate cycle tracks are common in most towns and cities. Some are good, others awful. You're not obliged to use them, even when they're going your way. Not all drivers appreciate this but it is so. If a cycle lane or track helps, use it. If it doesn't, don't. Be aware that on-road cycle lanes can put you further towards the kerb than safety dictates. If you leave a cycle lane, treat it like changing lanes on the main carriageway: look back, signal, move.

Cycle tracks off the road, perhaps along an adjacent footpath, present a different problem: you'll have to give way at every side road, whereas on the main carriageway you'd have right of way. Not only will that mean you progress more slowly, it also presents greater risk. It's at junctions where the vast majority of cycle accidents occur, and specifically T-junctions. That said, it can be pleasant to get away from the traffic on busy roads.

Some cycle tracks use extinct transport corridors such as old railway lines and towpaths. These go point to point without having to give way for roads. Many are shared-use and are popular with pedestrians. If so, give way as necessary and ring your bell to announce your presence. Look out for dogs being walked, particularly if the dog is loose or on a very long lead. Dogs don't know the Highway Code.

KNOW YOUR ROAD USER

Everyone has their bête noir on the road. White van man. School-run mum. Boy racers. BMW drivers. Cyclists! Try to avoid thinking in stereotypes. Other road users are just other people. If you can see them, be seen by them, and communicate with them, you are already half way to being a happy road cyclist.

A common refrain from drivers to cyclists is "Sorry mate, I didn't see you." That's why you take the lane when you need to, signal boldly, and

6.2 Cycling in traffic

Check behind before any change of position on the road. At junctions or when overtaking parked cars, get into position early rather than pulling out at the last moment. Photo: Cycling Images

look them in the eye. You're helping drivers see you. Even then, some drivers are distracted or careless and may not register you or the speed at which you're travelling. There are warning signs: the car might be creeping forward; the pitch of the engine may change; maybe there's a thumping bass beat that says there's a young male driver – statistically the most dangerous – at the wheel.

Drivers of long vehicles are often very skilful. Yet they may genuinely not see you because their vehicle has blind spots. If you cannot see the driver's face in one of the mirrors, the driver cannot see you. Don't cycle too close behind and NEVER cycle up the inside. The biggest risk isn't from the biggest vehicles, but from skip lorries and concrete lorries that race about urban areas on a tight schedule. Give them a wide berth. Watch out for bus stops ahead, in case a bus overtakes and pulls in suddenly.

Pedestrians can easily see you but may step out in front of you because they haven't heard you. Bikes are almost silent and pedestrians get used to gauging traffic by sound. This is where a ping of your bell comes in handy. If there's too little time to reach for your bell, shout 'Look out!' This usually roots the pedestrian to the spot while they work out just what it is they are supposed to be looking out for. You can then swerve past safely.

Motorcycle and moped riders may jostle for position with cyclists in urban areas, particularly filtering past stationary traffic. Riders of big motorcycles have to pass a test and are skilled. Riders of mopeds or small engine motorcycles may have passed compulsory basic training, but don't count on it. It *isn't* always compulsory if you hold a full driving licence.

Other cyclists should be no problem on the streets. Those that ignore traffic law are. Keep a close eye on cyclists riding along pavements or ignoring traffic signals. They might do something else equally stupid that puts themselves in your path.

You won't encounter horse riders very often. If you come up from behind, ring your bell some way back or call out 'Cyclist!' The silent approach of cyclists can spook horses, so it helps if the rider is forewarned.

PLANNING YOUR ROUTE

Riding a bicycle is one of the fastest and easiest ways to travel around a town or city. The reason? Cyclists have a reliable average speed. Capitalise on this when you plan your routes. You don't have to take 'fast' main roads that run directly from A to B. A more roundabout route down empty backstreets without traffic lights may be quicker, and will likely be more

pleasant. A section of cycle track or tow-path, or even a bit where you have to get off and walk, may still save time. Or it may just take you away from heavy traffic or a tricky junction that you'd like to avoid.

"A more roundabout route down empty backstreets may be quicker, and will likely be more pleasant."

A good cycling map can turn a nerve-jangling urban ride into an enjoyable experience. Some councils are enlightened enough to publish cycling maps of their cities; ask at the local Tourist Information Centre. If they don't, CycleCity Guides (www. cyclecityguides.co.uk) have cycling maps for a large number of towns and cities. If there isn't one, you'll need to experiment using the local street map.

If you take a wrong turn, don't worry about it. Don't hesitate. Go with it and pull over when it's safe. When you're stationary on the pavement you can get your bearings and look at your map. If need be, push your bike to where you want to get to if it's easier than riding there.

Before making any new urban cycling trip as a family – the school run, say – it helps to do a dry run by yourself. That way you can test how long it might take and see what the conditions are like. Maybe there's an easier alternative route?

Even young children can cycle safely on the road when chaperoned by a parent riding behind. Traffic awareness doesn't develop until later, so it's important your child can follow instructions. Photo: Cycling Images

Road cycling for children

SOME PARENTS WILL balk at letting their children near roads with traffic, let alone on them. It would be foolish to pretend there are no risks involved. However, at some point your child will use roads alone – if not on a bike then as a pedestrian or behind the wheel of a car as a young adult. Those who are used to independence and who can make risk assessments will be safer, better road users than those who have been isolated from the outside world. It doesn't require leaping in at the deep end. Exposure to traffic is something best done by degrees.

CO-RIDERS AND PASSENGERS

To begin with your child will travel on the road under your direct control, either as a passenger in a seat or trailer or as a co-rider on a tandem or trailer-cycle. As steering and braking are under your sole control, the only impact will be on how you cycle.

You will inevitably ride in a less swashbuckling style. Mostly it's because you are always more careful when kids are around; it's human nature. Partly it's because a heavier bicycle takes longer to get up to speed and to slow down, so your riding benefits from being smoother and less stop-start. Try to anticipate junctions by arriving slowly and in the right gear for setting off. Allow the extra second or two you'll need to pull away when judging gaps in traffic.

If you scrupulously observe the rules for solo cycling, you can cycle safely with children on quite busy roads. Nevertheless, quieter routes are better. They're simply more pleasant. You can chat easily if you're not drowned out by traffic noise, and an enjoyable trip will give your child positive associations with cycling rather than negative ones. So what if the quiet route is a bit further or takes five minutes longer?

A child on a tandem or trailer-cycle may pick up some traffic skills from you. You can reinforce this by asking an older child to see if there's anything behind and to signal left or right when needed. (You will still have to do both these things yourself.)

Tandems remain useful up to the age of 11 and possibly beyond. By that age, though, most children will want to ride solo. One reason is image. The desire to conform becomes very strong and children don't want to be seen as 'different' by their friends. The tandem that was once so popular may now be seen as geeky.

Even when you're chaperoning on a solo bike, it's worth looking at things through your child's eyes and maybe making one or two concessions. Riding with your pre-teen son on an urban mountain bike will likely be acceptable, even cool. Riding a small-wheeled folding bike while wearing luminous trouser bands may be highly embarrassing. Only you can decide where to draw the line here.

CHAPERONED CYCLING

Traffic awareness develops around the age of 8-10 years old, which is not coincidentally when school-based cycle training tends to start. Up until that time, at least, you will need to supervise your child on roads. He or she might be a proficient cyclist and yet make misjudgements about traffic.

Before setting out together there are some things you need to be sure of. One is that your child can stop, start, steer and otherwise be competent at cycling – on a bike that's roadworthy. Another is that your child will respond to your instructions, doing what you say when you say it. Do explain the reasons for this in advance: that you're not being bossy or cross, just careful. The final requirement is that your child knows the difference between left and right. When you say 'go left' it's important your charge doesn't cycle into the centre of the road instead…

When you're riding, it's best if your child leads and you cycle a bike length or half a bike length behind. That way you can watch your child at all times and call out instructions. Your child should ride towards the left side of the road, but at least 50cm out from gutter, while you ride further out, possibly taking the lane. This means traffic has to come around you and can't cut in too close to your child, who might veer or wobble or simply be freaked out by cars passing too close.

If you need to do so it is perfectly legal to cycle side by side with your child. (Many drivers are unaware that cyclists can ride two abreast, so be prepared for the odd pipped horn.) It's worth moving forward to ride alongside as you come up to a side road. Two cyclists are more visible than one, and with both of you to pass, any side-road driver is less likely to engage in the brinkmanship of edging or accelerating out in front of you. Some chaperones like to move forward to ride on the inside of the child at side-roads, which is fine too.

On quiet roads, conversely, you may wish to relinquish the lane and ride directly behind your child. This gives your child the opportunity to look behind to check for traffic, without having you in the way. It's not essential, since you're covering the job of traffic observer anyway, but it is good practice.

Give encouragement as you ride along and make your instructions calm and clear. Information should flow both ways. In particular, you child should be taught to say 'Stopping!' rather than halting right in front of you without warning. Ideally, your child should also signal left before pulling in to the side. (No one uses the one-armed up-down flap that signifies slowing down nowadays, and it may only confuse drivers.)

If there are two adults, the child or children should ride in the middle with an adult front and back. If there are two children to one adult, it's best if the more competent child cyclist leads, followed by the other child, followed by the adult. A skilled child cyclist can ride behind you, leaving you free to concentrate on just one rider in front.

Start on easier, less trafficked roads and work up. There will be situations in which it is easier or necessary to get off the bikes. Perhaps a hill is too steep. Perhaps a junction is too complex. In time your child will be able to ride these. For now, take it one step at a time. And remember: communication, communication, communication. After the ride, accentuate the positive. Too much 'don't do this', 'don't do that' can be a real downer when you're eight years old.

> "No one uses the one-armed up-down flap that signifies slowing down these days, and it may confuse drivers"

INDEPENDENT CYCLING

Independent cycling means riding on the road. Cycling on the pavement is illegal. There is no criminal liability for children under the age of 10, and it is tacitly accepted by everyone that the pavement is where younger children will ride. By the age of 11, however, and perhaps two or three years earlier, children can learn to ride safely on the road without supervision – not on all roads but certainly on roads that aren't busy and don't have complex junctions.

Cycle training has traditionally taken place in the later years of primary school. Not only are children ready for training then, they will soon need it. The average distance from home to secondary school is 3.3 miles in England – too far to walk, but not difficult by bike. Add in a wider catchment area for friends and, depending on public transport options, children will need to cycle if they're to get about independently.

Training has moved on quite a way since the cones-in-the-school-playground days of the Cycling Proficiency Scheme. The new National Standard for Cycle Training, which is funded by the Department for Transport and Cycling England, takes place largely on the road in real-world, supervised conditions. And the training itself is no longer administered by schoolteachers but by qualified, accredited cycle trainers.

There are three levels to the training. Level 1 is for beginners and covers basic cycle control skills, such as starting, stopping, manoeuvring, signalling, and using the gears. It takes place away from roads and traffic.

Level 2 is an introduction to on-road cycling, and that's where the training largely takes place. It covers skills such as positioning on the road, turning left and right, and overtaking. By the end of it, participants should have the

Cycling training is now administered by professional, accredited cycle trainers. Photo: David Dansky

ability and confidence to tackle short commuting journeys.

Level 3 teaches existing cyclists how to travel on any road. It covers more advanced skills such as roundabouts, filtering, complex turns and junctions. The emphasis is not so much on physically riding the bike – which participants will know – but how to make journeys by bike confidently and effectively.

You can find your nearest National Standards training provider at www. ctc.org.uk/cycletraining, or call the helpline on 0870 607 0415. Training costs from £15 per person per session, but it depends where you live. Local

6.3 Road cycling for children

authorities sometimes provide free or subsidised training. Your nearest training provider can fill you in about charging policy.

HOME SCHOOLING
Strictly speaking it isn't essential to have any training to ride a bicycle on

"Your child may pick up some skills from you through the osmosis of cycling together. Don't depend on this"

the road, inasmuch as it's not a legal requirement. It is, however, a practical requirement and it should not be overlooked. If you're unable to arrange training with an accredited National Standards cycle trainer, it's something you need to take charge of.

Your child may pick up some skills from you through the osmosis of cycling together. Don't depend on this. You will need to check. The best way to assess cycling ability is to shadow your child on a journey. This is like chaperoning except that you're not giving instructions and you're riding directly behind. You're just there to observe, and to step in if necessary.

You're looking for a number of key skills. Bike control is probably a given by this point, but do monitor things like the ability to ride one-handed and to ride without veering while looking behind. On top of that, check:

- Traffic awareness. Your child must look behind before changing position on the road and before slowing down. Try holding a certain number of fingers in the air for a few seconds to check if he or she is really looking.
- Communication. Using eye contact, positioning and signalling, your child needs to be able to communicate intentions clearly to other road users.
- Junctions. Explain who has priority and what the best way is to go through a given junction. Use real world examples.
- Positioning. Your child might not want to take the lane. It's easy to get bullied out of doing so by following traffic. You can nevertheless drill in the requirement to ride a good way – 50cm or more – out of the gutter.
- Bike awareness. Show your child how to check if a bike is roadworthy. Brakes work? Tyres firm enough? Quick releases done up? Nothing loose? Note that 'roadworthy' also means lights and a rear reflector at night. You're not expecting your child to fix any problems, just to alert you if there are any and not to head out the door on an unsafe bike.

As teenagers get older, they will want to be more independent. They won't want to be chaperoned or even shadowed. Nevertheless, it's worth doing dry runs yourself of any journeys that you know they will make. That way you can still offer practical suggestions about what to watch out for on the journey, or on alternative routes.

Photo: Martin Breschinski, courtesy of Transport for London

Cycling to School

WHILE NEARLY ALL children have bikes, less than one per cent cycle to school. It's not because they don't want to. According to a survey by the National Children's Bureau, 31% of pupils want to ride to school.

So what's stopping them? The main barriers are concerns about cycling in traffic, primarily from parents but also from children, and about the security of the bike at school. Some children also worry about the amount they have to carry to school each day.

Where these issues are addressed the results can be dramatic. At Kesgrave High School in Suffolk, 61% of pupils cycle to school – as many as in Holland or Denmark. With cycle training, better facilities, and a pro-active attitude from the school, other schools could emulate that success.

GETTING THERE

Cycle training is vital in producing competent, confident cyclists. It enables pupils to cycle in from all across the local area, not just along traffic-free corridors such as off-road tracks. There's always a road between two points, whereas access to cycle routes depends on where you live.

That's not to say traffic-free cycle routes aren't popular with parents and pupils, or that they can't have a big impact on numbers cycling to school. They do. Cycle-path charity Sustrans is doing excellent work in providing such routes (www.saferoutestoschools. org.uk), as well helping foster a pro-cycling culture at schools.

If cycle routes are not available or not convenient, don't judge the journey to school by the route you might take in the car. There's quite likely a better one for cycling, using back streets or traffic-calmed roads.

Luggage for school journeys can be heavy. A school bag has to be portable on the bike and on foot around school. For light loads, a small backpack or shoulder bag can be okay. Heavier loads need to go a rear carrier rack. Spring-loaded clips or single luggage elastics aren't really secure enough to hold a heavy school bag or briefcase safely on top of a rack. You need something like the Delta Cargo Net (£5, www.ctcshop.com). Alternatively, a single pannier with a shoulder strap would work. That could be a dedicated office pannier or simply a universal pannier such as the Ortlieb Front Roller classic (see Chapter 4). A second universal pannier could be used for sports gear/packed lunch/rain gear, assuming there's a locker available for your child to store it in at school.

AT SCHOOL

Legally, schools cannot stop children arriving by bike. The choice of how to get to school and the liability for the journey (for anything other than transport organised by the school

Many more children would like to ride to school than actually do. As well as cycle training, children require secure cycle parking facilities and a supportive school and parents. Photo: Cycling Images

itself) falls to you, as parent. However, schools can ban bikes on the premises, which makes cycle parking a problem.

Cycle parking has to be convenient, secure and in view from the main building(s) to prevent vandalism and theft. Rickety bikesheds won't do. The bikes need to be protected from the weather and supported securely by a proper stand, not a wheel-bending concrete or wire slot. For more ideas on cycle parking that works – to take to the next PTA meeting, perhaps? – see www.cycle-works.com.

Your child will need a lock, of course. There will be a trade off between portability, price and weight. A U-lock that's at least Sold Secure Bronze is recommended. Remind your child to remove anything that isn't fixed to the bike when it's parked.

Schools vary widely in their support for cycling. Those that are making the biggest strides in raising the numbers of children arriving by bike have one thing in common: there's always someone pushing for improvements. That someone could be you. Maybe you could press for lockers to be installed at school, if they're not available? Maybe you could become an accredited cycle instructor? It's a four-day course, with two assessed sessions afterwards. Funding may be available to pay for some or all of it. See www.ctc.org.uk/cycletraining.

TRANQUIL FOREST TRACKS or blurry-fast rocky descents: a mountain bike will take you there. An escapist 'fun bike' with fat tyres and a rugged build, it was born in California in the 1970s when cyclists customised old cruiser bikes for off-road, downhill thrills.

The mountain bike is now the default bike in the developed world. Different specialisations for everything from tricks and jumps to racing have branched off from the basic design. For the average weekend rider, however, the ethos hasn't really changed: it's still about messing about in the woods, getting muddy and sometimes falling off, and letting adrenaline and exercise push your cares away.

Children love it, once they've developed the strength and skills to cope with the terrain. There are lots of mountain bike routes with big drops and twisty, bumpy trails that require unblinking focus and not a little skill. Teenagers love these. Yet there are also off-road routes that suit families: they're short and the tracks are wide and not too rough. A 16-inch wheel child's bike or an adult hybrid will readily cope with such terrain, as would a trailer-cycle. It's still an escape into the countryside away from towns and traffic but the emphasis is on where you are rather than the technical demands of the trail itself.

To help you find the right type of track, off-road centres increasingly use a route-grading system like that in skiing. It ranges from Green ('easy', suitable for families and beginners) through Blue and Red to Black ('severe', suitable for expert mountain bikers). For more details, follow the 'Where can I cycle?' link at www.ctc.org.uk/mtb.

Dedicated trail centres aren't the only places you can ride off-road. You can also ride on bridleways and byways. In Scotland you have even more freedom. Surface conditions and topography vary greatly once you get away from roads, so it's worth doing a dry-run of any off-road route yourself before you take the kids on it.

As with trail centres, the rougher tracks require different skills from road-riding. If you ride like you're on a road a mountain bike will buck you off when the going gets choppy. You have to stand on the pedals and move your bodyweight around to balance. You brake differently. And you have to cope with conditions you'd never see on even the worst road. It's challenging – but fun!

Where to ride off-road

'OFF-ROAD' IS A WIDE definition that takes in every route that doesn't involve tarmac and motor traffic, from Sustrans trails through to rocky singletrack. Here we're focusing on unsurfaced routes.

These trails fall into two categories: purpose-built mountain bike tracks and 'natural' routes such as bridleways. Ultimately, all routes are man-made rather than natural, even if the trail builders were men and packhorses hundreds of years ago. The distinction is between routes made for mountain bikers and routes that cyclists happen to be able to use.

BRIDLEWAYS

Cyclists can use any public right of way except for motorways, footpaths and footways (footways are pavements next to roads). In terms of off-road cycling, bridleways are the most important. As the name suggests they were created by and for horse riders, but since 1968 cyclists have been able to use them too, thanks to lobbying by CTC. A cyclist has to give way to horse riders and walkers on bridleways.

Britain has thousands of miles of bridleways. To see what's available in your area you need a good map: either a 1:50,000 Ordnance Survey Landranger (2cm to 1km) or a 1:25,000 Ordnance Survey Explorer (4cm to 1km). As families are likely to travel shorter distances, the latter is better.

See www.ordnancesurvey.co.uk or go to any bookshop.

Bridleways are shown by a line of long pink dashes on a Landranger and by long green dashes on an Explorer. Get a highlighter pen and mark them all on your local map. You can create some excellent rides by linking up sections of bridleway. You might also

> "You can create some excellent rides by linking up sections of bridleway. You might also want to use unclassified roads"

want to use unclassified roads, byways open to all traffic (BOATs), and roads used as public paths (RUPPs), which are also shown on OS maps.

If you're riding in Scotland, the situation is different. The Scottish Outdoor Access Code says that you can ride almost anywhere so long you do so responsibly – for example, leaving an area as you found it. Exceptions include private gardens, crop fields and of course buildings. See www. outdooraccess-scotland.com for more.

Bridleways vary tremendously, and even looking at a map it won't be obvious what the riding conditions will be like. There are some clues. Bridleways in valley bottoms and on flat land can be muddy, whereas ones that cross contour lines should be

Children love scrambling around on their bikes off-road, but even more than on tarmac routes it pays to keep rides fairly shot. They can always re-ride their favourite bits if they finish the ride fresh. Photo: istock

better drained and drier.

Bridleways that run down the middle of a colourless track (dashed lines means unfenced, solid lines means fenced) tend to be wider and better surfaced. They might even be tarmac with a strip of grass down the middle, particularly if there's access from the track to a building. A blue horseshoe on an Explorer map indicates horse riders. Horses' hooves churn up soft ground, which can make cycling difficult.

The only way to be sure what a bridleway will be like is to ride it yourself. Some are fantastic green corridors through the countryside. Others are technically demanding to

ride. Others still are impassable unless you shoulder the bike and walk.

WATERWAYS

Canals have towpaths from the days that barges were pulled by horses. Many of them are suitable for cycling. There are also anglers, boaters and dog walkers to share the space with, and as with bridleways you're expected to give way. Progress can therefore be slow. Like bridleways, conditions vary. Some are narrow or muddy while others are so overgrown as to be impassable. For obvious reasons, it's important that everyone in your family can swim. Bridges reduce sightlines and the damp cobbles underneath

them can be slippery.

To cycle on a towpath you usually need a permit. This is free, however, and you can download it from www. waterscape.com. The site also shows recommend cycling routes by waterways across the country.

Since canals are old industrial routes, towpaths go right into the heart of towns and cities. This makes them excellent escape routes from urban areas.

TRAIL CENTRES

Visiting a mountain bike trail centre is the equivalent of going to a ski resort. You can choose from a selection of way-marked trails that are graded by difficulty level. There are usually toilets and there may be a café, bike shop and hire outlet on site too.

Compared to 'off-piste' mountain biking, trail centres have more uniformity. Similar purpose-built features crop up on different trails. Yet there is also more bang for your buck: purpose-built trails cram in a lot of technical thrills into a smaller area. The routes are tried and tested, and the way-marking means you can focus on riding rather than navigating. Most are great fun and justifiably popular.

Trail centres are a relatively new phenomenon. The UK's first opened at Coed y Brenin in North Wales in the mid 1990s. Others have followed across Wales and Scotland and, to a lesser extent, England.

Most trail centres are in forests. The Forestry Commission has created

Forests are great places for family riding, with everything from tranquil tracks like this to sinuous singletrack. Photo: Stockfile

more than 2,600km of waymarked cycle trails. You can search an online database for routes near you: www. forestry.gov.uk/cycling. Forestry commission routes use the Green to Black grading system.

Green routes ('easy') are suitable for beginners and families. They're fairly short, without strenuous climbs, and the riding surface tends to be wide forest tracks. Any bike will cope – even one with a trailer-cycle or child-seat. Blue routes ('moderate') are longer and hillier, but most are still suitable for reasonably fit families riding sturdy hybrid bicycles.

Red routes ('difficult') are mountain bike trails that you need a proper mountain bike and a good level of fitness and riding skill to enjoy. There will be challenging climbs and descents, and trail hazards such as drop-offs, roots, and steep, cambered corners. The trails tend to be longer, too. Black routes ('severe') are for experienced, skilled mountain bikers. Climbs and descents are steeper, the route could be longer, and the trail hazards are harder to negotiate.

With any route, the difficulty level will vary depending on your speed. The faster you travel, the harder the trail becomes – and vice versa: you can go more slowly around routes you're only just ready for, getting off and walking around trickier sections.

Take it easy at first. If you go skiing for the first time, you start on the nursery slope and work your way up. When you start mountain biking, you need that same kind of progression.

MOUNTAIN BIKING HOTSPOTS
Here are *some* of the UK's off-road hotspots. Trails are usually free, though car-parking may not be.

WALES
Afan Forest Park (near Port Talbot). 22km Green rail-trail route, three Red trails (15km-23km) and a Black (46km). Developing fast. Good facilities.
Coed y Brenin (near Dolgellau). A new Green route (10.8km) has been added to its collection of three Reds (8.7, 18.4 and 20.2km) and two Blacks (31.1 and 38.2km). Great facilities for families
Cwmcarn (near Newport). 15km

Red trail with an optional 1km Black section for expert riders.
Gwydyr Forest (near Betws y Coed). The Marin Trail is a 25km Red route. Penmachno, a few miles south, is a 22km Red route.
Llandegla (near Wrexham). 5km Green route, 12km Blue, 18km Red, and 21km Black.
Llanwyrted Wells. Lots of mapped bridleway routes from the town. Short (4-5km) Blue, Red and Black trails at nearby Coed Trallwm, Abergwesyn.
Machynlleth. Mach 1, 2 and 3 are 16-30km bridleway routes south of the town. Cli-machx is a largely Red 15km loop with a fast Black final descent.
Nant-yr-Arian (near Aberystwyth): 9km Blue trail and 16km and 35km Red routes.

You can find more information at www.mbwales.com.

SCOTLAND
Ae (near Dumfries). 9km Green route with optional 4.5km Blue extension, and a 19.6km Red route. There's also a 1.6km downhill route.
Dalbeattie (near Dumfries & Castle Douglas). 11.5km Green route, 14km Blue and a 27km Red that includes optional Black sections.
Fort William (between Torlundy and Spenn Bridge). Highlight is the 8.5km Red route, with Black optional sections, which was devised for the 2007 World Championships. Also has two Blue routes (1km and 19km) and a 16.5km Red.
Glentress & Innerleithen (near

Red-grade routes like this one – the Marin Trail in Gwydyr Forest, North Wales – demand a good level of fitness, a proper mountain bike, and the skill to use it. Even keen teenagers should try something easier or shorter to begin with. Photo: Dan Joyce

Peebles). The jewel in the 7stanes crown. 1.5km Green 'skills loop', 4.5km Green route, 8km or 14km Blue, 17km Red, 19.4km and 29km Black routes, a free-ride skills park, and four extreme downhill routes. Excellent facilities.

Glentrool (near Newton Stewart). 9km Blue route. There's also an ungraded forest/minor road route: the 58km Big Country CTC Ride. Seasonal facilities.

Golspie (between Inverness and Wick). 0.9km Green route, 6.5km Blue, 7.5km Red, and a 13.6km Black route.

Kirroughtree (near Newton Stewart). 6km Green route, 10km Blue with two optional extensions (+4km and +2km),

17km Red route and 31km Black. Good facilities, including play area.

Laggan Wolftrax (near Newtonmore and Kingussie). 4.8km Green route, 15km Red and 6.4km Black. There's also a 3.6km bike park trail.

Mabie (near Dumfries). 8.2km Green route, 10km Blue, 17km Red with optional 2km Black-graded extension. Also has a free-ride skills park for jumps etc. Good facilities.

Newcastleton (between Carlisle and Hawick). 0.4km Green route, two Blue routes (5.5 and 8km) and a Red (10.5km). There's also a short Black-graded North Shore section.

7.2 Where to ride off-road

For more details go to www.forestry. gov.uk/scotland and follow the 'mountain biking' link.

ENGLAND

Aston Hill (near Wendover). 9km Red route and a range of Red/Black downhill courses. There's an 8km Green trail in nearby Wendover Woods.

Avon Timberland Trail (Ashton Court, Bristol). 11km ungraded route.

Bedgebury Forest (near Royal Tunbridge Wells). 10km family route (Green), 12km Red-grade route, plus a skills area. Also has bikes/facilities for disabled riders.

Cannock Chase (near Rugeley). 11.3km Blue route, plus a leisure cycling route (also Blue) that's 1.6km-30.4km long.

Dalby Forest (near Pickering). Two Green routes (3.2km and 9.7km), 12.9km Blue, 37km Red and 9.7km Black. There's also a skills area and a downhill track. Good facilities.

Delamere (near Chester). Two ungraded trails, 6.4km and 11.3km, and a skills area.

Forest of Dean (near Monmouth). 17km Green route on former railway lines and a 4.5km Red.

Grizedale (near Hawkshead). Three Blue routes (3.2km-11.3km) and three Red (16km-22.5km). Good facilities.

Haldon Forest (near Exeter). 4.8km Green route, 3.7km Blue route and 11.3km Black route.

Hamsterley Forest (near Bishop Auckland). 4.8km Green route, three Blue (1.6km-14.5km), 22.5km Red and an 11.3km Black. Good facilities.

Kielder (between Newcastleton and Bellingham). 11.3km Green route, three Blue (0.8km-16km), three Red (15km-48km) and one Black (2.4km). Good facilities.

Penshurst Off-Road Club (near Royal Tunbridge Wells). Variety of short cross-country courses, jumps and downhills. Better for teens than tinies.

Queen Elizabeth Country Park (between Petersfield and Horndean). Two 6km ungraded routes.

Sherwood Pines (near Mansfield). 4.8km Green route, 9.6km Blue and a variety of short Black routes, including a 'Dual Descender' and a 2.4km

> "If you go skiing for the first time, you start on the nursery slope and work up. Mountain biking is the same"

training circuit. Good facilities.

Surrey Hills (near Dorking). Variety of ungraded but mostly intermediate or harder singletrack around Pitch, Leith and Holmbury Hills.

Swinley Forest (near Bracknell). Surprising variety of short, ungraded trails that range from easy to hard.

Thetford Forest (near Thetford and Brandon). 9.7km Green route, 12.9km Blue, 17.7km Red and a 16km Black.

For a more definitive list of places to ride in the UK, get *Where to Mountain Bike in Britain* by Nicky Crowther (£12, www.wheretoMTB.com).

Off-road skills

CTC Mountain Bike Skills Instruction starts simply but can do wonders for both your riding ability and your confidence. Some sessions are women only. Photo: Dan Joyce

IF YOU CAN RIDE a bike you can ride an off-road Green route. As trails become progressively steeper, bumpier, looser-surfaced and more hazard-strewn, different skills from riding on road are required. The guidelines here should get you and your children started but are not a substitute for experience or training.

Until your child is on a 24-inch wheel bike, any off-road riding will be fairly gentle. From then on, he or she may be able to tackle segments of Red routes. I say segments, because while children often pick up off-road skills

quickly they may lack the endurance for a longer ride. It's best to choose your trail sections and shortcuts by riding the route yourself in advance.

When you ride together you will generally ride behind. You can't tell what's happening if you're in front, and it can be hard to look back on a narrow, bumpy track. It is sometimes useful to lead to demonstrate how to negotiate a certain part of the trail. Behind is usually better. You can see what your child is doing, give instructions, and are on hand immediately if required.

Before you set off, make sure all the bikes are not just roadworthy but off-roadworthy. A malfunctioning brake or loose quick release could cause a serious accident.

GENERAL PRINCIPLES

Don't sit on the saddle like a sack of potatoes. You have to stand up on the pedals quite often off-road. Partly that's because there are steep climbs that you'll need to power up, as you would on road. There are two more important reasons why you have to stand up on a mountain bike. One is so that you can move your centre of gravity around to keep your balance. The other is so that you can use your bent arms and legs as shock absorbers, to minimise the impact of bumps. Arms and legs can absorb bigger bumps than bicycle suspension but they do single hits better than a rapid succession of bumps, which quickly become fatiguing. The more suspension travel you've got on the bike, the less bump absorption your body will have to do.

Stay loose. If you lock your arms and legs and hold onto the handlebars in a death-grip, bumps and vibrations will come straight through the bike into you. The bike becomes a bucking bronco that could easily kick you off. If you're out of the saddle, knees bent like a jockey, hands firm but not white-knuckled, you ride the bike instead of the bike careering away with you on top of it.

You go where you look. It's the same principle as for younger children learning to ride a bike for the first time. Off-road, however, there are more obstacles. It's easy to get distracted by that tree stump in the middle of a trail. Look past it. Focus instead where you want to go. Look along the trail on the imaginary line that you will be following. That's where your wheels will then go. It helps to keep your head up too – so you're looking ahead rather than down.

Whatever skill you're trying, start small. Before charging down a hill on a Red route, try hanging off the back

"The more suspension travel you have on a bike, the less bump absorption your body will have to do"

of saddle while descending a grassy slope. It will look weird, like a downhill skiing position on a nursery slope, but it will get you used to the idea before you have to implement it. Similarly, practise riding over a drop-off that's a few inches high before you tackle anything bigger.

Adjust your brakes. Set the levers so that they're a bit more horizontal, that is: just below the level of the handlebar. This relaxes your arms and wrists, moves your weight back a little and lifts your head up. All these things will improve you ride by increasing comfort and – because your position is better – confidence. With children's bikes, and sometimes women's, you may also need to adjust the reach of the brake levers to suit smaller hands.

STEERING

Bicycles are steered not just through the handlebars but through the hips and shoulders, by leaning. The faster you go the more you steer by leaning and the less by turning the bars. On

> "Most of your actual stopping power comes from the front brake. However, you need to apply it progressively"

road you'll do this unconsciously. Off-road you may need to remind yourself.

Practise standing on the pedals – keep them at ten to three, so they're level – and use your hips to move the bike around underneath you. Try this on a grassy slope. Put a couple of markers down so you can slalom between them.

At slow speeds, balance and steering become harder. Yet the slower you are able to cycle, the less often you will stall on the trail and be forced to dismount. It's possible to come to a complete stop balanced on the bike, with your pedals level and your front wheel turned into the slope. It's called a trackstand because it's used by cyclists on velodromes – also known as tracks. Being able to cycle really slowly is useful for picking your way through

difficult terrain, especially while you're climbing.

CORNERING

Watch a racing driver go round a corner on a Formula One circuit. The driver starts wide, cuts in across the apex of the bend, and finishes wide. It makes the bend a shallower angle. The same technique works for the same reasons on a mountain bike.

As in car, it upsets the handling if you brake on a bend. You don't need to 'power around the bend' on a bike – you just need to keep your wheels turning. So do the bulk of your braking, and ideally all of it, before the bend. Then release the levers so that your wheels can roll rather than skid around the curve. Don't overuse the front brake or grab at it on a steep or fast bend.

As you go into the bend, lean the bike over and put your pedals at six o'clock with your outside pedal at the bottom of the stroke. This gives the leaned over bike more pedal clearance as you corner. Pushing down with your outside foot (on the pedal that's at the bottom of the stroke) helps the tyres dig in a bit and so gives better traction.

Don't look down into the corner as you go into it. Instead, look at your exit from the corner. Remember: you go where you look. The more you can keep your focus on a point along the trail ahead of you rather than the point where you are right now, the smoother your riding should be.

Try to avoid cornering on a slippery

When descending, stand on level pedals and keep your weight back. Cover your brakes but don't snatch at them. This is a skills instruction session and it's the rider's first time on this slope. Good effort! Photo: Dan Joyce

surface, like thick mud. You want to ride in as straight a line as possible, pedalling in an easy gear.

DESCENDING

For freewheeling downhill, the default position is: level pedals; bum off the saddle and pushed back a bit; knees and elbows bent; one or two fingers of each hand covering the brake levers. The steeper the slope, the further back your centre of gravity – that is, your backside – needs to be. If it's really steep, you need to hang your backside right off the saddle, just above the back wheel, with the saddle up by your chest and your arms out straight. If it's not too steep, just keep your weight back – perhaps gripping the saddle between your thighs for stability.

It's easier to get your weight back and down if you lower your saddle, which is why some bikes have a quick-release lever on the seat-tube. Once you've lowered the seat-post there's more room to move around.

BRAKING

When you're braking on a bike you normally use just the forefinger and middle finger of each hand. If you've got hydraulic disc brakes, it's possible to use only one finger. Either way, you can keep the rest of each hand wrapped around the grip so that it won't be bounced off the handlebars.

The limit of your ability to slow down isn't the power of the brakes so much as the traction of your tyres. You can lock a bicycle wheel with just about any brake. Best avoided. If you're skidding you're not in control. Instead of snatching the brakes, periodically squeeze the levers to keep your speed down. A gentle touch – 'feathering the brakes' – might be enough.

Which brake to use? Both. Most of your actual stopping power comes from the front brake. However, you need to apply it progressively rather than grabbing at it and to keep your weight back. The rear brake just helps to keep your speed down.

Avoid the temptation to slow down too much on a steep slope, as you're likely to stall. A bicycle that's moving forward is more stable than one that isn't, and if it's rolling a little faster it's even less likely to fall over. Momentum is your friend.

CLIMBING

What goes down has to go up, sadly. You can always get off and push, but with practice most climbs can be ridden. Short climbs can be 'rushed'. You attack them at speed, pedalling out of the saddle as you start to climb, and hope you don't run out of gas before the top.

For longer climbs you will need to pace yourself and to go down through the gears. Get in the right gear as you approach the climb. If you find yourself pedalling too slowly, change down. Don't wait until you can barely turn the pedals. You need to ease off the pedalling pressure a little to change gear and you can't do that if you're grunting your way up a climb.

Given a low enough gear, it's possible to get up most climbs sitting on the saddle. Keep your head up, your wrists relaxed and drop your heel into the pedal stroke. Keeping your wrists loose and dropping them slightly stops you pulling on the bar and lifting it, while dropping the heel as you pedal helps drive your power through the back wheel rather than lifting it. Try to breathe normally and don't fight the slope. Look through the climb: don't just focus on the summit. Spinning the pedals rather than slowly cranking them keeps the bike moving when the terrain is loose or steep.

If the slope is too steep, or if your legs start to ache too much, you'll need to pedal standing up. This is less efficient in that it uses more energy, but it still delivers more power and it does so using slightly different muscles. If your bike has suspension, it's easier to pedal out of the saddle if you can lock it out, otherwise some of your energy will go into activating that.

Climbs with a rocky or rooty surface are especially hard. It's easy for the front wheel to be balked or to hit a bump and come upwards off the ground. The rear wheel, meanwhile, may scrabble for traction and

Photo: Cycling Images

7.3 Off-road skills

wheelspin to a halt. It helps to pedal smoothly and to keep some weight over your rear wheel. A slightly softer rear tyre also aids grip.

BUMPS AND JUMPS

Look at a mountain bike magazine cover and you might think that it was essential to spend a good deal of time in the air when riding off-road. Well, no, not really. Even most Black routes can be ridden wheels on the ground. It's only skills parks and downhill runs where you're meant to be in the air. On less difficult routes, it's your choice. So here's the careful parent's guide to bumps and jumps.

Drop-offs are a common feature on

Getting both wheels off the ground – while maintaining control of your bike – requires practice. Photo: Cycling Images

Red routes as well as Black. A drop-off is a big step down. You can roll over ones about as high as your front wheel (but don't start with ones that high!). You need to get your centre of gravity back as you go through the drop-off. Keep your weight back. Dropping your wrists and heels helps as it pivots you back on the on the bike. Keep your head up and focus on where you're going rather than where you are. Keep your breathing normal, so that you stay relaxed. Approach the drop-off at an easy pace, standing on level pedals, and as the front wheel nears the lip of the drop, get your weight back. The front wheel will land, compressing the fork, and you'll roll through.

Humps are common in trails too. Skilled riders use them as launch pads. If you'd rather not, you can 'swallow' the bump. Approach it out of the saddle on level pedals, weight around the middle of the bike rather than way back. As you rise up the bump, bend your elbows and knees so that the bike comes up towards you and you're crouched over it. As you go over the bump – but not before – shift your weight backwards so your weight balance is right for the down-slope. If you go into a jump with your weight back, you will take off.

Should you find yourself in the air by accident, don't panic. If you look right down in front of you, you'll pivot the bike that way and nosedive. Keep your head up and look out along the trail – or even upwards – and try to drop your heels and pivot your wrists down.

This should keep the bike level and you'll land wheels together.

ADVANCED TECHNIQUES
Jumping isn't the only time you might get a wheel or two in the air. Lifting the front wheel up enables you to roll over trail obstacles better. There are two ways to do it: without pedalling,

"Experience isn't the only teacher. There's no faster way to learn to ride than by getting proper instruction"

which is known as a manual; and with pedalling, which is a wheelie.

Performing a manual isn't a matter of hauling on the handlebar. You 'weight' and 'unweight' the front end of the bike by pushing down and through the handlebar and moving your weight back. As you push down and through with your hands, stand up off the saddle on level pedals, leaning back, dropping your heels, and pushing your bodyweight down and through the bike. With the front wheel unweighted, your lean will lift the front wheel. Skilled riders can find their balance point and roll along on the back wheel, but to begin with just getting the front wheel up is enough.

A wheelie adds pedalling into the equation. While it's easier to get your front wheel up, it's also easier to pedal your back wheel past your balance point. With practice, either technique

is useful for clearing small logs or potholes; the back wheel can simply roll over or through.

You can also use a manual or wheelie to launch off drop-offs too, so that you land your wheels together. It's essential to do this if you're travelling too fast to roll over the drop-off or if it's too high. I wouldn't recommend it except on small steps to begin with.

'Bunny-hopping' lets you clear trail obstacles completely. This means getting both wheels in the air. Get the front wheel up as you would with a manual. Then you need to unweight the rear wheel by first pressing down and through on your heels to weight it. Then you unweight it and spring up. It's easier said than done, but it's a neat trick if you can pull it off. If not, you can always get off and lift the bike over the obstacle!

SKILLS INSTRUCTION
Experience is a good teacher but it isn't the only one – or even the best. There's no faster way to learn how to ride a bike off-road than by getting proper instruction. Use a coach with a recognised qualification, such as a CTC Mountain Bike Skills Instructor. CTC is developing a national network of instructors with training centres across the UK. For more details, see www.ctc.org.uk/mtb.

Different skills courses are suitable for different riders (some are women only) or age ranges (some aren't suitable for children) so be sure to match the session to your party.

Trail tips

MOUNTAIN BIKING burns around 500-700 calories per hour. It also makes you sweat. To keep going for more than an hour or so, you'll need food and water. Lots of energy bars and drinks exist. You don't need to bother with them unless you're racing. Simple water is fine, and for food any carbohydrate-rich, low-fat snack is a reasonable top-up fuel. Good choices include cereal bars, malt loaf, dried fruit, fig biscuits, bananas, and jelly babies.

The amount you need to drink will depend on the weather and your size. And some people just drink more than others do. Around 500ml per person per hour of riding is reasonable. If you're not using a hydration pack, expect to carry a couple of 750ml plastic bike bottles – it's better to have too much than too little.

TRAIL ESSENTIALS

Being further from shops and shelter means you need to carry other things with you when riding off-road, as well as snacks and water. Take a cheap, pay-as-you-go mobile phone (that way it doesn't greatly matter if it gets broken). You can't always get a signal – try up high, above the tree cover – but it's better than looking for a phone box.

What else you take will be dictated by how remote the area is that you're riding in. On a trail centre or a local bridleway, I'd carry:

- Map (trail centre map or Ordnance Survey map)
- Compass
- Multi-tool
- Puncture kit
- Two tyre levers
- Pump
- Spare innertube
- Spare chain links
- Cable ties
- Spray-on Elastoplast
- Small immobiliser lock for café stop
- Cash
- Spare wind- and shower-proof top
- Spare insulating layer for my son(s)

All this fits in one small capacity hydration pack, except the compass, which happens to be a bell on the handlebars. With more than one

> "Lots of energy drinks exist. You don't need to bother with them unless you're racing. Simple water is fine"

child, I use a larger pack for the extra spare tops/jerseys and an extra innertube. The children just carry water and snacks.

Some riders like to add: space blanket; small torch; whistle; Ibuprofen or paracetamol; bandages. Don't forget to let someone know where you're going too.

TRAIL SAFETY

A helmet is essential for mountain biking. Cycling mitts or gloves offer protection to the hands in a spill. If you or your children are riding on flat pedals rather than clipless ones that hold your feet in place, there's another useful bit of protective gear for trickier trails: leg armour. 'Flat' pedals are spiky and can take divots out of your shins in the wrong circumstances. It's easy to catch a knee in a fall, so you may as well get combined shin and knee armour – or perhaps just the knee armour if you're on clipless pedals. SixSixOne (www.sixsixone. com), RaceFace (www.raceface.com) and Dainese (www.dainese.com) all make good sets, including ones small enough for 11- or 12-year-olds. Try them for size in the shop; fit varies. Expect to pay from £30/pair.

Different sections of armour exist and if you get the lot and add in a full-face helmet you end up looking like a Power Ranger. But if pushing your limits on technical trails is what you or your teenager enjoys, it's the way to go.

The most effective way to avoid injury, of course, is not to fall off. That means riding what you're comfortable riding at a speed you're happy with. If it's too hard, walk it. When walking the bike down a steep slope, have the bike on your right if you can. You can then use your left hand to hold the left hand grip and apply the rear brake. With your right hand, hold the saddle. This way the bike won't run away from you as you walk down.

You can get through 500ml of water an hour while mountain biking, so a hydration pack is handy. Photo: istock

IF SOMEONE HAS A FALL

Most falls don't result in serious injury: the fallen rider is simply bruised, grazed and/or winded. Let the rider just sit for a while. A sip of water or a snack can improve spirits. Clean any cuts with a squirt of water from your hydration pack and apply a bandage or spray-on plaster. Don't set off immediately. Take stock of any sore areas, make sure the bike is rideable, then shortcut the ride as necessary.

If the situation is more serious, have one person stay with the fallen rider while the other phones or fetches help. First aid training is a real asset in such a situation. Try St John Ambulance for training: www.sja.org.uk/training.

Photo: Dan Joyce

RIDING A BIKE IS A GREAT WAY to explore the countryside. As when you're walking, you're in the scene in surround-sound outdoors where you can feel the breeze and smell the air. It's much nicer than looking at it through glass. When you're cycling you travel slowly enough not to miss anything and quickly enough to go some distance, through changing environments. It's a simple pleasure that costs practically nothing and that anyone can enjoy.

Requirements for touring are minimal. If you can ride a bike to the shops you can ride it to the next village or across the whole county. Some cycle-tourists cross countries or continents. All you really need is a bike and the desire to go somewhere. There's no minimum or maximum speed, duration or distance; no age limit; no special skills or unusual equipment needed; and no rules. You could cycle the local lanes with a bottle of water and a flapjack one afternoon, or you could take a family-sized tent and cycle-camp across France one summer.

It's not about the destination so much as it is about the journey. You want to follow the nicest route between two points rather than the shortest. That usually means getting away from the busiest roads and instead using minor roads and traffic-free cycle tracks – and sometimes bridleways and towpaths (see the previous chapter).

Family cycle touring begins with the family bike ride. You get on your bikes and go for a ride for a couple of hours. Travelling further is only slightly more difficult in that you will need to sort out a place to stay for the night. You'll need to take more things with you, and perhaps you'll be cycling further. That doesn't mean the riding need be any more strenuous; you can potter along at whatever pace you please, which with children might be quite modest. It doesn't matter. If you wanted to travel quickly you could jump in a car.

Extending a trip from one night to a long weekend or a fortnight is hardly any more difficult than continuing to pedal. The logistics of sorting beds for more nights and of carrying a bit more luggage are only slightly more involved than doing the same for one night. But you don't have to do even that. If you prefer you could go on an organised cycling holiday – like a package holiday – where all the travel arrangements are done for you and your one job is to ride.

Family bike rides

A FAMILY BIKE RIDE is about more than pedalling, just as any day trip is not solely about the journey. For younger children, a small park with play equipment or an open space for kicking a ball around is fine. Maybe there's stunning scenery, a viewpoint with picnic tables, or just a nice café or family-friendly pub? Or perhaps you could combine the ride with a visit to a castle, beach, museum, country house, ancient monument, or the cinema?

Whatever you choose, err on the short side for your first few rides together, especially if you're the keen cyclist and everyone else is fairly new to cycling. If it's further than you could ride in an hour, it's probably too long. Molehills to you could be mountains to your family and your meagre distance could be their taxing ride.

That's true of small children on their own bikes, where five or 10 miles is an achievement, but also to a lesser extent of children on the back of tandems or trailer-cycles, and possibly your partner. Until a few rides have given you a more reliable guide, assume your average speed will be no more than 5mph (including short, unplanned stops). If you make better time than this, it's not a problem. It's better to

Quiet roads are just as pleasant for touring as off-road routes. When you unfold your OS Landranger, plot your ride on the white and yellow roads as far as possible. Photo: Sue Darlow

underestimate. You don't want the ride to become an unpleasant endurance exercise. You can always extend trips up to 20 or 30 miles, or even further, as time goes by.

There are a few things you can do to help level out your riding speeds, so you're not accidentally drifting off the front. First, make sure the child-seat/child-trailer/trailer-cycle is on your bike. Secondly, you should carry the luggage yourself – everything from spare jumpers and jackets to the toolkit and picnic. Lastly, change down to a really easy hill-climbing gear so that you're 'speed limited'.

CHOOSE YOUR ROUTE

A good map is the most valuable touring accessory. In a car you can follow road signs to get where you want to go, but as signs are designed for motor traffic they will guide you down the biggest, quickest roads. Those are the last places you want to be! With a detailed map you can plot your own route from A to B via lanes, tracks and back roads.

Harvey (www.harveymaps.co.uk) and Goldeneye (www.goldeneyemaps.com) do some very nice maps for cyclists for areas of the country popular with tourists. The best maps with nationwide coverage are by Ordnance Survey (www.ordnancesurvey.co.uk). The 1:50,000 Landrangers are more useful for cycling on roads than the 1:25,000 Explorers you might use off-road, because each map covers a greater area: a chunk of the country 40km (25 miles) across.

On Landrangers, main roads (A roads) are coloured red – apart from the even busier 'primary routes' (also A roads), which are coloured

"That's the essence of touring: enjoying the journey, not minimising the journey time"

green. Plan any route to avoid both as far as possible, especially primary routes. Busy roads make touring feel like commuting, and if you're accompanied by less confident cyclists even a few miles on one can spoil your day. Use minor roads (coloured yellow or white) or, when they're unavailable, B roads (coloured orange).

Since the shortest point between two places will usually be linked by the biggest road, this will often mean taking a longer, more roundabout route. But that's the essence of touring anyway: enjoying the journey, not minimising the journey time.

Of course, roads aren't your only option. Sustrans' National Cycle Network is a 10,000-mile (and growing), UK-wide web of signed cycle routes. While two thirds of the network is on minor roads, the rest is traffic-free thanks to segregated cycle tracks, canal towpaths and reclaimed, disused railways. Around 75 per cent of the population is within two miles of some part of the National Cycle

8.2 Family bike rides

Network. The on-road sections make for good leisure rides, while the traffic-free sections are ideal for families or cyclists who aren't confident with cars.

Visit the Sustrans website at www.sustrans.org.uk to find what's available near you. There's a searchable map. Sustrans' online shop sells many guides to particular areas of the NCN. If you want an overview of the whole country, then Traffic Free Cycle Trails by Nick Cotton (£13) is recommended. It contains over 400 route ideas.

Many bridleways and towpaths are suitable for family day rides too (see Chapter 7). Check by yourself first. Some are pretty rough and require a mountain bike, while others are impassable except by walking through foot-deep mud.

BE PREPARED

For a short ride, where you set off from home and come back again, you may not need any amenities. In other circumstances, you might want car parking, toilets, or somewhere to have lunch. Your map will give you some idea of what's there on the ground, but it won't tell you what's open. Try the nearest Tourist Information Centre or research the information online.

Better still: do your research in person. If you can reconnoitre the route beforehand, you'll know what to expect to a level of detail that no map or guide can match. You'll know about that tricky gravelly corner, the fact that you might spot deer in such and such a spot, or that there's a café serving hot chocolate just over the next hill. This knowledge can be invaluable.

Preparation doesn't end with the route. One of the hardest parts of cycling with small children is simply getting out of the door. It can feel like an expedition. Minimise morning prep time. The night before: check the bikes and equipment; make the packed lunch; lay out clothes; prepare a pannier or seat pack with tools, first aid kit, etc. If you have to fuss around fixing things before you set off, children get fractious.

At the very least, prepare the bikes the night before. Make sure that the tyres are properly inflated, that all bolts are tight, and that brakes and gears work okay. Better still, do this day before: that way you've got time to nip out and buy, say, a new innertube or brake cable.

Your bike will probably be in good running order if you use it often. Your family's bikes might not be. Mostly that's because you're not riding them, and a problem that you would correct could go unnoticed – and get worse.

WHAT EVERYONE WANTS

The more you can involve your family in the ride, the more they'll get out of it. Where does your partner want to go? Your children? Discuss the route options together. Use the map to talk through the realities of the route. This is useful during the ride too. If anyone's getting tired, it helps to be able to say: 'Look, we're nearly there. Lunch is just round this corner.'

You and your family may have different criteria for what constitutes a good bike ride. If your children are happy, however, you will be, so focus on what they want. Children are often more impressed with the cake they can have in the café than with nice scenery. A ride that's a washout because of the weather can be saved in their eyes when you bring out a surprise comic or a favourite toy. One of the strengths of cycling is that it's an activity the whole family can enjoy. That means it also provides an opportunity to talk to and listen to your children, in a way that hectic modern lifestyles leave little time for. It's precious one-to-one time, and your children may think more fondly of bike rides for that reason.

You can use the animatedness of your children's conversations as a barometer of how they're feeling on the ride. If they go quiet or start whinging, they're tired. Time to rest or have a snack. If it's harder than you thought – maybe it's hillier or the weather's against you – revise your route. Turn around. Take a shortcut. Quit while you're ahead.

The pace of the ride needs to be geared to the slowest family member. It's demoralising if you cycle ahead, wait at the top of a hill for the others, then immediately set off again. And it's just bad form. It's like putting six goals past your son in a back-garden game of football and celebrating each one.

So long as the children aren't bringing up the rear, it's easy to set your pace by theirs. It's even easier on traffic-free off-road routes such as Sustrans tracks. So long as you can still see your children, you can let them roam ahead. This lets them discover things first, and it automatically means that you're travelling at their pace. If anyone falls off or stops, you'll be able to react straight away.

Being in front, they have the opportunity to initiate any stops. And they will want to stop more often than you: for a drink, to have a rest, to say hello to the horse in the field, whatever. If they want to stop, stop. There's no rush. If the hill's too steep or the descent too technical, get off

Let your children lead the way. That means you'll automatically be going at their pace, not yours. Photo: istock

and push. Forget about cycling to get somewhere or to get an adrenaline buzz – smell the flowers.

Conversely, if everyone else is cycling along happily, try not to stop them too often for photographs. Ride ahead, stop, shoot them coming past, then catch up. Get your pictures when everyone's fresh – early on, after lunch, or at your destination.

DON'T LEAVE HOME WITHOUT IT

Day rides are not demanding in terms of equipment. So long as everyone is comfortable and has a bicycle that's suitable for the kind of terrain you'll be riding on, you're good to go. Having said that, don't forget:

- Plenty of drinks. Water in plastic bicycle bottles (750ml per person, or more) is best. It can also be used for washing hands or cooling down on sunny days, whereas juice can't.
- Snacks. Energy boost and morale boost in one. Fuel is much the same as for other forms of cycling: cereal bars, fruit, fig biscuits, cakes.
- Extra layers. Wind and showerproof jackets all round. Fleeces or jumpers for the kids for when you stop.
- Spare nappies/pants and trousers. For babies and just potty-trained toddlers. It will happen. Also a plastic bag for the wet stuff.
- Toolkit. Pump, tyre levers, puncture kit, spare innertube for each wheel size, multi-tool. Even if you're not a mechanic, you may meet a Good Samaritan who can help you out – if you've got the necessary equipment.

- 'First aid' kit. Plasters, antiseptic cream, painkillers, Factor 30 sun cream in summer, wet wipes. Plus any required medication.
- Mobile phone, for unlikely emergencies – preferably an old pay-as-you-go model so it doesn't matter if it gets lost or broken.
- Cash. You might not think you'll need it, but it's nice to have the option of buying ice lollies or cups of tea if they're available.
- Lock. Even it's just a lightweight immobiliser to run through the bike frames outside a café.
- Distractions. For the children – e.g. tennis ball, Frisbee, action figure.

FURTHER AFIELD

Day rides don't have to begin at your own back door. You can explore further afield by driving or taking the train to a different start point. It's not as convenient to reconnoitre routes like this, so the more information you can find out about your proposed route in advance from other family cyclists, the better.

Routes will probably be circular, like the rides you do from home. Linear routes are possible. If you're travelling by train, you can come back via a different station. If you're travelling by car, one parent can stay with the children – perhaps in a café – while the other rides back to pick up the car.

Car- or train-assisted riding can reach beyond the countryside that's an hour or two away. You could even take the bikes with you on holiday abroad.

Photo: Cycling Images

Cycle touring

WHEN YOU'RE CYCLING along with the sun on your back and the wind in your hair, it can be tempting to keep going instead of turning for home. Try it! That's cycle touring: extending your day's ride to the next day, or the day after that, or the next week. It's no longer just a day out or a bike ride: it's an adventure.

How self-sufficient you want to be will determine your luggage, and even the bike that you ride. If you're carrying your kitchen and your bedroom with you because you're camping, you'll need plenty of panniers and a bike that will accommodate them all. If you're 'credit card touring', you need only a day-bag and any bike will do.

A good target for your first trip is to pick an interesting destination 15-30 miles away, riding there on the first day and returning the next. A B&B or youth hostel is perhaps the best option, but just because you're a cyclist doesn't mean you can't stop at a hotel or a Travelodge. Prices for the latter are competitive when there's a whole family in one room.

CREDIT-CARD TOURING

Touring is easier the less weight you carry. You can travel further or faster, or just use less effort. At the extreme, this means you'll have only the clothes you stand up in, your credit card, plus whatever you can stuff in handlebar bag and/or seat pack – or a hydration pack if you're mountain biking. You stay in hotels or B&Bs and hand-wash your kit in the sink or shower each night, drying it on the radiator ready for the next day.

You have to be ruthless with what you take, paring it down to a monk-like minimum. It's a useful strategy if you want to travel light on road bikes, or if you'll be mountain biking from place to place. It's seldom ideal when you're touring with children, who will usually want home comforts like spare clothes and a toothbrush that

Two rear panniers will hold a lot of luggage but for family camping you'll need even more bags. Photo: Dan Joyce

hasn't had the handle cut off to save weight. The exception is on organised rides that have a sag-wagon (i.e. a van or minibus) to move your luggage between overnight stops. You can then have a suitcase of gear but carry almost nothing on the bike.

Younger children are unlikely to enjoy unsupported credit card touring. Teenagers might. Even then, it helps to have tried touring with more luggage a few times beforehand so you have a better idea of what you can do without.

You'll probably need 10 litres or more of luggage space per person. It's easier when there's more than one of you because you can share tools, toothpaste, etc. Here's one possible kit list. For when you're on the bike: helmet (if you use one); cycling glasses; mitts; wicking vest; short-sleeved jersey; Lycra shorts; socks; cycling shoes (ones you can walk in); arm warmers (extra warmth, minimal bulk); knee warmers (ditto); shower-proof gilet (ditto); pump; puncture kit; two tyre levers; spare innertube; multi-tool; cable ties; spare chain link or two; a pocket-sized cable lock; water bottle; snack(s).

For when you're off the bike: one or two pairs of pants; lightweight poly-cotton walking trousers or shorts; T-shirt; lightweight fleece or jersey (which can also be used on the bike); flipflops if you can't walk in your bike shoes; travel toothbrush & paste; small deodorant; sunblock; plasters; pain killers. You won't need a towel, soap or shampoo as the hotel or B&B

will provide them. You'll also want a map or a GPS for your route, a mobile phone, some cash, and of course your credit card. You may be able to squeeze in a luxury such as an MP3 player, a small radio, a deck or cards, or a

"How self-sufficient you want to be when touring will determine your luggage and even the bike that you ride"

paperback. Anything else you need, you buy en route. It sounds and is Spartan, but it's strangely liberating to travel with so few possessions.

TWO-PANNIERS TOURING
Sometimes called short-haul touring, or even just 'touring' since it's the most common type, two-panniers touring involves cycling through first world countries and spending each night with a proper roof over your head. The extra luggage space means the minimalism of credit card touring is not required, though your bike choice is pretty much limited to those that can be fitted with a rear carrier rack. (Some other combination of bags is possible, such as huge saddlebag or two panniers at the front.)

You need about 25 litres of luggage space per person and may want more. That's a couple of universal/front panniers or one big rear pannier each. One parent can easily carry one child's gear as well this way by using two rear

LEUKAEMIA RESEARCH

HODGKIN'S | LYMPHOMA | MYELOMA

LONDON
BIKEATHON

13 JULY 2008

- Five great circular routes
- Cycle 13, 26 or 52 miles
- A children's ride

CAN'T MAKE THIS DATE?

TAKE PART IN ONE OF OUR FAMILY AND CHILDREN'S BIKE EVENTS AROUND THE UK

SIGN UP TODAY AND HELP US FIGHT BLOOD CANCERS!

www.londonbikeathon.co.uk
www.lrf.org.uk/cycling
bikeathon@lrf.org.uk
020 7269 9097

Registered charity 216032 (England & Wales)
SC037529 (Scotland)

panniers, or two children's gear by using two rear and two front panniers.

Even though you've more room than the credit card tourer, it will still take practice to pare down your luggage to fit this space. So lay out all the gear you think you'll need and then get rid of the half of it that isn't essential.

A sample kit list might include the following. For when you're on the bike: helmet (possibly); sunglasses; mitts; Lycra shorts; tracksuit trousers or baggy shorts to wear over the top; wicking vest; T-shirt or cycling jersey; fleece; showerproof or waterproof jacket; socks; trainers or cycling shoes; same tools as the credit card tourer but more spares.

For when you're off the bike: three sets of underwear (one on, one off, one in the wash); lightweight trousers; T-shirt(s); body warmer; sandals; toiletry bag, including Vaseline (in case of chafing) and wet wipes. If you're staying at a youth hostel rather than a B&B you will also need soap, shampoo (sachets?), and a hand or travel towel.

As well as the map, lock and mobile phone (and charger?), you can take more luxuries – a camera, travel boardgame and book. If you're stopping at youth hostels, which have kitchens you can use, you can carry a few basic foods too.

WHERE TO STAY

The UK is blessed with lots of B&Bs and they tend to congregate in just the sorts of rural areas that touring cyclists like to explore. Price and quality varies widely and capacities are often small. Solo cyclists can turn up in any town and usually get a bed for the night. Family cyclists will need to book ahead.

Do spell out that you'll be arriving by bike, because you want somewhere secure and undercover to store your bikes. The star rating for hotels and B&Bs is just a guide; well-run establishments can score low due to a lack of facilities rather than a lack of quality or care.

For a list of cyclist-friendly B&Bs, visit the CTC website (www.ctc. org.uk) and follow the links 'What I need', 'Travel Services' and 'Cyclists Welcome Online Directory'. With these establishments, you know the owners are used to dealing with cyclists and that they'll look after your bikes.

Youth hostels are an excellent alternative to B&Bs. There are more than 200 in England and Wales, mostly in honey-pot touring areas. Virtually all of them have bike sheds. You don't have to be young or even a member to stay there. Costs are low because you stay in single sex dormitories in bunk beds, although families can book a room to themselves in most hostels. Prices range from £33 a night for a family room – about £8 per person! That doesn't include meals. Youth hostels often have breakfast and evening meals available. They also have kitchens and dining rooms – and pans, plates and cutlery – that any guest can use, so you can take your own food with you.

You will be provided with a sheet sleeping bag at a hostel, so you won't need bedding. You will need your own towel. If you'll be staying in a dormitory, take foam ear plugs – there's always one snorer. For more information about the Youth Hostel Association, or to join (which gives you discounts), see www.yha.org.uk. Don't forget that you can stay in hostels across the world, too.

Children under three are welcome in some hostels but not all. Children aged 14 or over can visit youth hostels by themselves, with parental permission.

CYCLE-CAMPING
Cycle-camping is the most self-

Cycle-camping can be hugely liberating, and it's a big adventure for children. Photo: Cycling Images

sufficient way to travel, and it's a great way to enjoy the outdoors. It's an expedition for children, whether you're spending one night at a campsite 15 miles from home or a couple of weeks touring through France. Once you've got the kit, it's a cheap holiday too.

The price of carrying your kitchen, bedding and shelter with you is an inescapably bigger load. The adult bike(s) will likely need four panniers each. Tent, groundsheet and poles may fit in a large rear pannier and/or across the top of the rear rack, but you'll still have sleeping bags and mats to carry somewhere. A luggage trailer adds capacity if you need more. Or you can fit a carrier rack to one or more of the children's bikes, so long as you don't overload them. Light items that are eating into adult pannier space are best: sleeping bags, showerproof jackets and such. However you pack, don't put tent pegs in with the tent as they may tear it.

A tent for family cycling needs to be much lighter and more compact that those huge tents you see in catalogues. You can get two small tents and pitch them face to face, with an adult in each or with older children in the non-adult tent. Or you could get one big one. Whichever way you do it, aim for a weight of under 2kg per person – and the lower the better.

If you're getting two tents, there's plenty to choose from tents designed for backpackers. If you're getting one big one, there's less choice, though a tent that fits three adults will usually fit two adults and two children. Tunnel tents offer more 'living space', while dome tents have more headroom. A tent with two entrances is best, because you can come in and out without walking past a lit stove. Alloy poles are better than fibreglass, which can break. Good family tents include:

- Saunders Space-Trek, sleeps four, 4.15kg, £269 (www.robertsaunders .co.uk)
- Nomad Amazon 3, sleeps three, 5.9kg, £280 (www.nomad.info/uk)
- North Face Bedrock 55, sleeps five, 6.15kg, £380 (www.ellis-brigham .com)
- Tatonka Alaska 4, sleeps four, 6.1kg, £275 (www.tatonka.com)
- VauDe Opera, sleeps four, 7.6kg, £330 (www.vaude.com)

You'll need a groundsheet too. And to insulate you from the ground and provide a bit more comfort, everyone needs a least a foam rollmat. Self-inflating Therm-a-rest mats (not a lilo: too bulky) are even more comfortable.

Down sleeping bags are very warm and compact but are quite expensive and take a long time to dry if they get wet. Synthetic bags are bulkier but easier to live with. You can pay silly money for mountaineering bags that you don't really need for a UK summer. That said, there's nothing worse than shivering through the night. I'd recommend a three-season bag so you stay cosy. Expect to pay from £40 upwards. Good brands include Mountain Equipment, Marmot, Vango, and VauDe.

For cooking, a couple of resealable gas-cartridge stoves will suffice. Alternatives include a meths-burning Trangia or, for those travelling further afield, a multi-fuel stove like the MSR Whisperlite. Whatever method of heating you use, get a reasonable sized cookset that includes 1-, 1.5- and 2-litre pans with lids. They stack inside each other like Russian dolls, and you can get a little kettle that will do the same. For eating, stackable plastic bowls, beakers and plastic cutlery are sufficient. Don't forget a dishcloth, a small amount of washing up liquid, and a tea towel. Two-pan meals based around pasta, rice or noodles are easy,

Children can carry one or two panniers, but give them light stuff to carry such as their own clothes. Photo: Sue Darlow

as are camp favourites like tinned beans and sausages. Experiment at home using your cookset on the kitchen hob.

Clothes will be much the same as for short-haul touring. Quick-drying material is best for obvious reasons, so avoid cotton. For children, a spare fleece and tracksuit trousers can double as pyjamas, and everyone's main jumper or fleece can be rolled up underneath the head of the sleeping bag for use as a pillow.

Towels take a long, long time to dry when camping. MSR's Packtowls (various sizes) take up little space and dry quickly (from £5, www.firstascent. co.uk). If everything does get wet, head for the nearest laundrette.

Tools will need supplementing with camp tools, such as a mallet for tent pegs and either a Swiss army knife or Leatherman for can and bottle opening. Either offers a way out of the tent if a catastrophe happens and it catches fire – you just cut through the side with a blade.

A useful extra for camping is an LED head torch or two, such Petzl's Zipka (£25, en.petzl.com). Use it for reading, going to the toilet block at night – even as an emergency bike light.

As with other places to stay, campsites can vary tremendously in quality, facilities and clientele. In the UK, look for Camping and Caravanning Club sites (www.campin gandcaravanningclub.co.uk) – they're good sites and you don't have to be a member to stay there.

PREPARING FOR YOUR TOUR

If you're a regular bike rider, you don't need to worry about training to go touring. Just don't over-commit yourself – or your family – for your first few days. They might manage 40 miles on day one but struggle to do any miles at all the day after.

Go easy and let your fitness build as you go. If you've over-estimated your daily mileage, reschedule your plans. As a rule of thumb, don't ride more than two-thirds the distance you would do as a one-off under the same conditions. So if you're used to doing day rides of 30 miles, don't aim to ride more than 20 miles a day back to back – at least, not to begin with. Plan to include rest days too.

Family touring is easier in flatter areas, so be careful what route you pick in Cornwall, Wales, the Pennines or the Scottish Highlands. Easier areas include East Anglia, the Vale of York, and the Scottish Borders. You can get free touring advice from CTC if you're a member (www.ctc.org.uk).

If you're planning a longer trip, have a 'shakedown tour' first. This is an overnight trip somewhere nearby. Load your bike up with everything you intend to take, do the daily

"If you're planning a longer trip, have a 'shakedown tour' first. This is an overnight trip somewhere nearby"

mileage you intend to do on your trip, preferably in similar terrain. Use this experience to add to or subtract from your kit list. Don't try anything brand new and untried – especially a saddle or shoes – at the start of a tour.

FIRST BIKE TRIP ABROAD

Whole books have been written about cycling in Europe – as they have on camping. There are lots fantastic places to visit, and it's possible to get there with a bike by various combinations of 'plane, train, ferry, coach, car and bicycle. You could cycle down the Loire Valley, explore the Black Forest, the Galician coast, or the hills of Tuscany... just for starters. Once again, CTC has a whole library of information sheets and route advice it can offer free to members.

For your first family trip abroad, I'd recommend keeping it simple. Take a ferry to Holland or Denmark. Both are excellent cycling countries. Hills are modest, the climate is much like the UK's, everyone speaks English, and both countries have a huge cycleway network. You don't even need the car; you can cycle straight onto the ferries.

To reach Denmark, take the overnight ferry from Harwich to Esbjerg with DFDS Seaways (www. dfds.co.uk). Stop at a few campsites or youth hostels ('Danhostels') as you travel out on one of the national cycle routes (1 or 8, maybe) then work your way back to the ferry port. If you want help planning your itinerary, contact De Frie Fugle (www.friefugle.dk), a Danish cycling organisation that's part of the European Cycling Federation. They are happy to help anyone sort out a cycle tour in Denmark. The Danish Tourist Board site, www.visitdenmark .com, may also be useful.

To get to Holland, there are ferries from Harwich to the Hook of Holland day and night. The journey with Stena Line (www.stenaline.co.uk) takes a little over six hours. Alternatively, take the DFDS ferry from Newcastle to Amsterdam, or the P&O ferry (www.poferries.com) from Hull to Rotterdam. Both sail overnight both ways. There are more bicycles per capita in Holland than anywhere else in the world, and the results of this are everywhere. You could take one of the LF cycle routes through Dutch countryside and towns. There's a map showing them all, the Fietsideënkaart (bicycle ideas map) for a few Euros from Dutch bookshops and ANWB ('Dutch AA') offices. You can get it online via www.fietsplatform.nl, but the internet shop it takes you to is Dutch only. The one down-side to cycling in Holland is that bike theft is relatively common, so take a good lock. For more information, see also www.holland.com/uk and holland. cyclingaroundtheworld.nl.

Don't forget travel insurance. Be sure the policy covers cycling and note that some policies won't include 'dangerous activities', which may include mountain biking. Insurance aimed at cyclists does exist. Take a look at www.cyclecover.co.uk.

A flat, cycling country such as Holland makes for easier cycle touring when your children are younger. Photo: Steve Melia

PACKAGE TOURING

Package touring costs more than doing it yourself, but you do get a tried-and-tested trip with full back-up, and usually a bit more luxury. Exactly what's included on an organised cycle touring holiday varies between holidays and operators, not least depending on how much you're paying. Many trips are 'self-led': that is, you get a route-marked map, which you follow to each night's pre-booked accommodation. Others have a guide who accompanies you. All have a support phone number you can ring if you get into difficulties, and some have a van that carries your luggage.

When you're considering an organised holiday, it's best to compare the price with other non-cycling holidays in the area. Just because you're on a bike doesn't mean that it will be cheap, any more than a holiday in which you lie on a beach – another free activity – ought to be cheap. A DIY tourer might sleep in a tent and live off pasta. When you're staying in decent hotels and eating three-course meals, the price will rise accordingly.

CTC has its own holiday company, CTC Cycling Holidays, which offers a huge range of cycle-tours in Britain and abroad. Some are specifically aimed at families, and the easier-graded ones are also suitable. See www.ctctours.co.uk for more.

All you have to do is pedal...
The ideal holiday for families

Cycle Spain
with
IberoCycle

Freephone: 0800 247 1831   Web: www.iberocycle.com

Great British rides

HALF THE FUN can be designing your own routes, yet there are plenty of off-the-shelf tours designed by other people, not least CTC – visit www. ctc-maps.org.uk. The ten rides here are just to kickstart your ideas. Many are traffic free, not because that's the only way to tour but because it's an easier way to begin. All are mapped, except the straightforward Bealach na ba circuit, and many are signed as well.

DAY RIDES

THE CAMEL TRAIL, CORNWALL
The UK's most popular tourist cycle route attracts 350,000 cyclists each year. It's a 17-mile ex-rail route beside the River Camel from Poley's Bridge to Padstow, via Bodmin and Wadebridge. It's ideal for younger children riding their own bikes or sitting in trailers, and while riding both ways is a long day out you can just ride from Wadebridge to Padstow and back, a 12-mile round trip. See www. visitcornwall.com.

HARTINGTON, PEAK DISTRICT
The village of Hartington gives easy access to three excellent old railway paths: the High Peak Trail (17.5 miles), the Tissington Trail (13 miles) and the Manifold Way (8.5 miles). Despite the Peak District hills, cuttings and embankments keep these trails mostly flat, although the High Peak is exposed in places. YHA Hartington Hall, a 17th century manor house, is a nice place to stop for families, and Alton Towers theme park is nearby. See www. visitpeakdistrict.com.

LÔN MAWDDACH TRAIL, NORTH WALES
The Mawddach Estuary is stunningly beautiful, with watercolour Welsh hills heaped up about a broad, peaceful estuary. The trip from Barmouth to Dolgellau is 11 miles each way, mostly along an old railway path. The pub at Penmaenpool part way does food. If you're here for a few days, the off-road trails of Coed y Brenin are nearby. See www.cyclingnorthwales.co.uk.

THE CUCKOO TRAIL, SUSSEX
An 11-mile ex-rail path from Heathfield to Polegate, with an onward link to Eastbourne. It runs through farmland and deciduous woodland, with interesting sculptures en route. Once again, it follows the route of a dismantled railway, making it good option for children on their own bikes. For a PDF leaflet, visit www.eastsussex. gov.uk and follow the links: Leisure and Tourism, Discover East Sussex, and Walks.

PUTNEY BRIDGE TO WEYBRIDGE, LONDON
Yes, touring in London. Escape the

hurly-burly of the capital into peaceful greenery. This 18-mile route runs mostly on riverside paths alongside the Thames and also takes in Richmond Park. For a shorter option ride from Kingston Upon Thames, which is nine miles from Weybridge. Sustrans' Thames Valley Cycle Route (London - Oxford) has all of this route and more. Get it from www.sustrans.org.uk.

LONGER RIDES

TAFF TRAIL, SOUTH WALES
This is a 55-mile largely traffic-free route from the middle of Cardiff up to Brecon, passing Pontypridd and Merthyr Tydfil en route. You don't have to cycle both ways as the Brecon Bike Bus connects Cardiff and Brecon on Sundays between May and August. Sustrans' Lon Las Cymru South map covers the Taff Trail and more. Get it from www.sustrans.org.uk. See also www.tafftrail.org.uk.

BEALACH NA BA CIRCUIT, NORTH WEST SCOTLAND
Explore the Applecross Penninsula, which is just across the sea from Skye. Cycle clockwise from Shieldaig, taking in Britain's most spectacular road climb – for which you will need very low gears. The 43-mile circuit could be done in a day by fit families with tandems or teenagers, or you could camp or B&B in Applecross. See www.undiscoveredscotland.co.uk/ applecross/peninsula/index.html.

COAST TO COAST, NORTHERN ENGLAND
Spend three or four days riding 140 miles across northern England from Whitehaven on the west coast to Sunderland on the east on minor roads and traffic-free trails. Around 12,000 cyclists make the trip every year, and the mapping, signage and facilities are accordingly good. Going west to east has the wind at your back (usually) and means short steep climbs and long downhills. See www.c2c-guide.co.uk.

THE SOUTH DOWNS WAY, SOUTH EAST ENGLAND
A 100-mile off-road chalk hills trail between Winchester and Beachy Head. It's not technically demanding in mountain biking terms but it does require a good level of fitness to do the whole thing. Allow three or four days, or just do bits of it. See www. nationaltrail.co.uk/Southdowns.

LAND'S END TO JOHN O'GROATS
Britain's ultimate big ride. Take three weeks to cycle a scenic 1,000-mile route from the tip of Cornwall to the top of Scotland, covering around 50 miles a day. Children as young as nine have ridden this on their own bikes, but it will be easier with tandems, or older children. CTC have an End to End information pack, which is available free to members. Non-members can buy it for £12.50 (cheque to 'CTC') to CTC Touring Department, CTC, Parklands, Railton Road, Guildford, GU2 9JX.

9.1 A well-oiled machine

YOU DON'T HAVE TO BE ABLE to take a bicycle apart to enjoy riding it, any more than you need to be a garage mechanic to drive a car. Yet there are some little jobs that need doing to keep either type of transport running at its best: adding oil, putting air in the tyres, washing it from time to time.

Even if you'd prefer to send your bicycle to the shop for servicing or repair, these weekly checks are tasks that require little in the way of mechanical know-how or specialist tools. They make a huge difference. Half-inflated tyres are much more likely to puncture and they sap your cycling efficiency, as does a rusty chain.

These are two of the reasons that cycling is sometimes perceived as hard work, instead of the magic carpet glide it ought to be. Other reasons could be that the 'hard-work bike' is a Bicycle-Shaped Object, or that the handlebars or saddle aren't in the right place, at the right angle or even of the type to suit the rider. Of course it's uncomfortable and tiring to ride a bike with a plastic saddle set nearly a foot lower than it ought to be. That's like complaining that walking is hard if you get about in a Cossack-dancer's squat – while wearing one-size-fits-all plastic clogs.

You or your bike shop can easily tweak and change your bike to make it fit like a glove. Remember: if it's not comfortable, it's not right. Accept no advice from anyone – however knowledgeable they seem to be – that makes you physically uncomfortable on your bike. One man's meat is another's poison.

If you are happy to roll up your sleeves and literally get your hands dirty then you'll find that bicycle maintenance is much more intuitive than car maintenance. Cars are complicated and the engine itself might as well be a magic box for all that most of us understand of it. Bikes aren't like that. Most of the moving parts are in plain view, and they use 19th century technology that you can easily grasp – in both senses of the word.

There isn't space in this book to look at bicycle maintenance in any depth. However, we'll look at how to prevent and cure that most common 'mechanical', the puncture, and provide pointers on a few other jobs and the tools you'll need to tackle them.

The right fit

A bike that's the right size for you will still need some adjustments to make it comfortable and efficient for you to ride. To fit the bike to you, rather than suffer by fitting yourself to it, you need to change the position of the bike's contact points relative to one another. These are the points where you connect with the bike – the handlebar, pedals and saddle.

The most important dimensions are the saddle-to-pedals distance and the saddle-to-handlebar distance. You may also want to change the contact points themselves, for something wider, narrower, longer, shorter or just more padded.

There is no definitive right and wrong, only what feels right and comfortable to you. In particular, feel free to ignore any bike-fitting formulae that you may read in more technical cycling books. These theories are just extrapolations of what people found tended to work for racing cyclists. They're not gospel, and their usefulness for utility and recreational cycling is moot.

SADDLE POSITION

Most people ride with their saddle set far too low. It's inefficient because you can't extend your leg muscles. Put on the shoes that you'll normally be wearing on your bike. Now, with the bike leaning against a wall or held up by a friend, sit on the saddle and put your feet on the pedals in the normal position – that is, with the ball of your foot over the centre of the pedal. Turn the cranks backwards until they are in line with the seat-tube. The leg at the bottom of the pedal stroke should be *almost* fully extended.

How much is almost? Repeat the above test with your heels on the pedals. One leg should be just about

> "Most people ride with their saddle set far too low. It's inefficient because you can't extend your leg muscles"

straight at the bottom of the stroke. Not stretching or straining and not bent, just straight. Now, when you put the balls of your feet on the pedals, ready to ride, your legs will be *slightly* bent at the bottom of the pedal stroke.

This is just a starting point. Less experienced riders, especially young children, may prefer the saddle lower so that they can get more than a toe on the floor when pausing at junctions etc. Mountain bikers sometimes have the saddle lower to be able to move around the bike better, while some road racers like it higher. It shouldn't be so high that your pelvis rocks from side to side. That can do nasty things to the neat stack of vertebrae in your

Saddle height for adults and older children is right when, with your heel on the pedal, your leg is just straight (left). When you put the ball of your foot on the pedal for riding, the leg is slightly bent at (and near) the bottom of the pedal stroke (right). Photo: Dan Joyce

back or, more likely, the discs that sit between them.

Moving the saddle up and down is easy. Just undo and re-tighten the seat binder bolt at the top of the frame. It will either be an Allen bolt or a quick release lever. Make sure you don't exceed the 'maximum height limit' on the post, which will indicate that there's only a short section still in the frame. If the saddle still isn't high enough then you'll need a longer seat-post.

As well as up and down you can also move the saddle fore and aft, albeit only by 3-5cm. You may need to do this to fine-tune the saddle-handlebar distance, which is known as reach. Your bike probably has a micro-adjust seat-post with a single big (6mm) Allen bolted clamp that grips the saddle rails. Undo this and you can slide the saddle backwards and forwards to get the saddle to where it's most comfortable. Make sure this bolt is nice and tight when you're done. Otherwise, if you go over a bump when you're sitting down on the saddle it can come loose.

Undoing the saddle bolt also lets you tilt the saddle. To begin with, set it dead level. Some cyclists, especially racers, prefer to tilt the nose of the saddle down by a few degrees. That's okay, but bear in mind that it will put more weight on your wrists and hands. Don't have the saddle pointing

9.2 The right fit

upwards. It will compress the nerves in your perineum, which can lead to pain or numbness.

If your bike has a plain seat-post then the clamp is integral to the saddle. There will be big (e.g. 13mm) nuts either side of the saddle base. Undo each of these a small amount at a time, until you can move the saddle as above.

If the saddle itself is uncomfortable, change it. For short distances in an upright position, you need a fatter, softer saddle because it's carrying all of your weight. For riding faster and further in a more leaned over riding position, the saddle is more of a perch than an armchair and needs to be thinner and harder. See also Chapter 5.

A stem riser puts the stem much higher, while the butterfly handlebar reduces reach. Photo: Dan Joyce.

STEM

The stem connects the handlebar to the steerer tube at the top of the fork. Stems come in a variety of lengths and angles, so you can have the handlebar just where you want it. Changing the stem length affects the steering a bit – with a longer stem your hands will move through a larger arc than they will with a short stem, so you'll have to move your hands further. This will make the steering feel 'slower'. But it's not that big a deal and within the limits of a bike that's your size to begin with it's nothing you can't get used to. Getting the contact points in the right place for you is more important.

As a general rule of thumb, you want the top of the handlebar about as high (or higher than) the saddle, unless you're a sporty rider looking to ride fast. Try touching your elbow to the nose of the saddle and reaching forward towards the handlebar with your hand. On a bike that fits, the horizontal distance from your fingertips to the stem's handlebar clamp will likely be between two and four fingers' width.

You can change the height of the handlebar by moving the stem up or down the steerer tube. If you have a stem that clamps to the outside of the steerer tube – a threadless stem – then there will be spacer washers below and/or above the stem itself. The stem can sit anywhere between, on top of or under these washers. If you're leaning over too much, put the stem at the top of the stack, and vice versa.

To change the stem position, undo and remove the top cap. Loosen the bolt or bolts that clamp the stem to the steerer and lift it and any washers off. Slot them back on in your preferred order – the stem or top washer should overtop the steerer tube – but only do up the stem bolts loosely. Refit and tighten the top cap. Make sure the stem is in line with the front wheel and tighten its bolt(s) fully.

To change the height further with this kind of stem, you can flip it the other way up when you re-fit it (in which case, you will also have to refit the handlebar). Or you can buy a new stem with a steeper or shallower angle. It's also possible to buy a 'stem riser' – a bolt-on extra bit of steerer tube.

Some bikes have a stem that clamps the steerer tube internally with a wedge bolt. Such stems look a bit like a number seven and are called quill stems. There's usually a greater range of height adjustment than with threadless stems. As with seat-posts, you should not exceed the maximum height marker.

To raise the stem, undo the Allen bolt on top. To free the wedge inside, you will probably need to give the bolt (or Allen key) a smart tap with a wooden mallet. You can then move the stem up and down. When it's at the right level, hold it steady while you tighten the stem bolt. Again, make sure the handlebar is in line.

Some bikes have an adjustable-angle stem. Both threadless and quill types exist. The advantage of such stems is not so much that you can change the position of the bars from ride to ride, but that there is a greater range of handlebar adjustment. Once you've found a position you're happy with, you could buy a sturdier, lighter rigid stem with the same dimensions.

HANDLEBAR
More width equals more leverage and easier control, but it also makes you less aerodynamic. Drop bars should be about the width of your shoulders, flat bars whatever you're comfortable with. It can get expensive if you want to switch from drop bars to flat ones because the brake and gear levers will need changing too.

Drop handlebars don't fix your hands in one position, so you'll probably have no complaints – try cork or gel bar tape if you need to improve comfort. With flat or riser bars your hands have just one position. Different bars will change the height of the handgrips, with riser bars giving you an extra bit of height – like having a taller stem. Different bars can also have a different upward or backward sweep, changing the angle at which you hold your hands. You can also add clamp-on bar ends to give you an extra hand position. Cane Creek's Ergo Grip bar ends are recommended (£30, www.extrauk.co.uk).

Butterfly or trekking bars are another way of getting multiple hand positions on a 'flat' handlebar. In particular, they're useful for reducing reach since the ends loop back from the stem clamp.

Bike care

PREVENTION IS BETTER than cure. If you keep your and your family's bikes in good condition then you'll have fewer problems to deal with. Check the bikes every week or two and give each an annual overhaul, either personally or via the bike shop.

If you want to go beyond the basic checks described here, you'll need a book that's solely about cycle maintenance. *The Haynes Bike Book* (£15, www.haynes.co.uk) is pretty good, as is the *Big Blue Book of Bicycle Repair* by Park Tool (£18, www. ultimatepursuits.co.uk). Or you could get yourself a video guide, such as The Bike Inn's *General Maintenance and Roadside Repairs* DVD (£22.50, www. bike-inn.co.uk).

Many tasks aren't technically demanding but make a big difference. Chief among them are keeping your tyres pumped up firm and oiling the chain. Soft tyres and a rusty chain are inefficient, and soft tyres also make bike handling poor and increase the risk of punctures.

Innertubes slowly leak air so you'll need to top up your tyres every couple of weeks. There will be a pressure rating on the side of the tyre, such as 6-7bar or 85-100psi. (1bar = 14.5psi.) The lower figure is your minimum. Get a floor pump with a pressure gauge and it will be effortless to keep your tyres topped up.

There are two common valve types: Schrader (like a car tyre) and Presta, which requires a narrower pump grommet. With a Schrader valve, you just remove the valve cap, press the pump head onto the valve, and flick the pump's locking lever to hold it in place. With a Presta valve, you also need to back off the little top nut on the valve as far as it will go before you start pumping (screwing it down after you've finished). If you're using a hand pump, hold one hand around the pump head and tyre to prevent sawing the valve back and forth.

If you're still plagued with punctures

> "If you're still plagued with punctures even with firm tyres, don't be tempted by solid tyres. They are truly awful"

even with firm tyres, don't be tempted by solid ones. They are truly awful. Try a sealant like Slime in your tyres (www.slime.com) or use tyres with Kevlar or similar puncture protection. Toughest for town use are Schwalbe Marathon Plus tyres (£27.50, www. fisheroutdoor.co.uk).

A wet chain rusts. After any wet ride or washing, dry the chain with an old rag or a piece of kitchen roll. Then apply a water displacer such as WD40 or a PTFE lube to the chain while you turn the cranks backwards. Spray each link as it comes out of the rear derailleur. Let it stand for a while, then wipe off any excess.

ESSENTIAL BIKE CHECKS

You won't need to do these checks on your own bike every time you go out on it, because you'll get used to hearing and feeling when things need attention. They're really useful for your children's bikes or your partner's, which you won't have been riding.

Start with the front wheel. Is the tyre firm? Lift the bike by the handlebar or stem so the wheel is just off the ground. Turn the wheel, checking the tyre for damage, and then spin it to make sure it isn't buckled and that

the brake isn't rubbing. It shouldn't wobble side to side by more than 2-3mm. Before you put the bike down, hit the top of the wheel with your palm to make sure it doesn't drop out of the fork. Put the bike down and make sure the hub's quick release lever is done up, or that the axle nuts are tight if it uses those instead. Hold the top of the wheel and try to rock it side to side to check for play.

Move up to the handlebars. Squeeze the front brake fully on – the lever should not touch the handlebar – and push the bike forward, so that the back wheel starts to come up into the

> "You won't need to do these checks every time you go out – you'll get used to feeling when things need attention"

air. With both wheels on the ground, try rocking the bike backwards and forwards while you hold the front brake on. If there's play then the headset probably needs tightening. Then squeeze the rear brake lever and move the bike forwards. The back wheel should skid. When you squeeze each brake, check that the rim brake blocks hit the middle of the rim squarely.

When the brake is applied, you can see the end of the cable where it goes into the lever, so check it's not frayed. Next, grip the front wheel between your knees while you stand over the

Use a floor pump with a pressure gauge to keep your tyres inflated to the figure printed on the sidewall. Photo: Dan Joyce

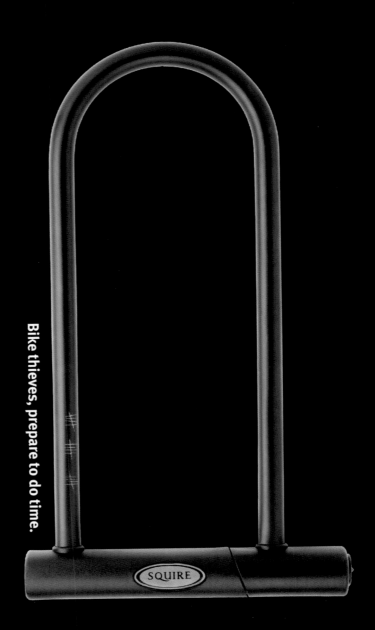

Bike thieves, prepare to do time.

Lock it, Leave it, Keep it

front of your bike and try to twist the handlebar side to side. It shouldn't move. Each end of the handlebar needs a grip or end plug; an open tube could apple-core you in a crash.

Move down to the transmission. Pedals should not be loose or bent and should turn easily. Hold the cranks with your hands and check for play by rocking them from side to side. To check the gears, you need someone to lift the back of the bike up. (If you're on your own, you'll need a workstand.) While you turn the cranks forward with one hand, click through the rear gears with the other. Each click should shift the chain one sprocket over. If

it doesn't, the gear cable tension may need adjusting. Send the chain from the top to bottom sprocket and back again. If it won't shift onto a sprocket or shifts the chain off the cassette completely, you'll need to tighten (to move less) or loosen (to move further) the set screws on the derailleur: the one marked H sets the derailleur's outer limit, the one marked L its inner limit. Repeat with the front shifter and derailleur. Make sure the chain runs freely. If it skips, there could be a stiff chain link.

On a bike with hub gears, click through the gears to make sure each is available and doesn't allow the cranks to slip forward and 'pedal air'. The chain on a bike with hub gears or a single-speed gear shouldn't be drum-tight but nor should it be slack. If you can move the upper run of chain up or down more than a couple of centimetres then it's too loose.

Move up to the saddle. Try to twist it side to side and up and down. The saddle itself should be level, or nearly so, and the seat-post should not have its 'maximum height' marker exposed.

Move down to the rear wheel and make the same checks as on the front wheel. When you've finished, you'll have checked the bike over in an M-shaped pattern: front wheel, handlebar, transmission, saddle, rear wheel. For that reason, this is called the M-check. Finally, check all fittings – everything from reflectors to mudguards to carrier racks – to make sure nothing is loose or rattly.

Hold the front wheel between your knees and check that you can't twist the handlebar. Photo: Dan Joyce

9.3 Bike care

WHEEL REMOVAL

You need to be able to get the wheels off your bike to fix a puncture. It can also be necessary when transporting your bike, whether it's in a large, padded bike bag or the back of a car.

If your bike has rim brakes rather than disc brakes you will first need to unhook the brake so that the tyre can fit past the brake blocks. To unhook a V-brake, use one hand (i.e. not the lever) to squeeze the brake onto the rim. With your other hand, pull the J-shaped metal 'noodle' out of the yoke that's attached to one of the brake arms. Sidepull brakes have a cam lever on one side of the brake; release this to gain some slack.

If you are removing the front wheel, you can now turn the bike upside down, resting it on its handlebar and saddle – unless you have a workstand. For the back wheel, first change gears so that the chain is on the smallest chainring and smallest sprocket, and then turn it over.

Undo the wheel's quick release lever or back off the large track nuts. For the front wheel, you will also need to back off the knurled nut on the opposite side of the quick release lever in order to clear the safety lips on the fork drop-outs.

The front wheel can simply be lifted out. To remove the back wheel, pull the rear derailleur back against its spring so that it's out of the way, and pull the wheel up and forward (or down and forward if the bike is on a workstand the right way up).

On a bike with a single-speed rear wheel, you need to slide the wheel forward in the drop-outs when you've undone the quick release/wheel nuts to get some slack in the chain. You can then unship the chain and lift the wheel out. Hub-geared rear wheels are trickier. You need to disengage the gear cable and sometimes undo a torque arm that's bolted to the frame. Procedures vary. Consult a manual or your bike shop.

To refit the front wheel, slot the axle into the drop-outs – and the disc rotor into the calliper if your bike has disc brakes. With wheel nuts, tighten each nut with your spanner, working alternately a turn or half a turn at a

If your bike doesn't come with quick release levers on the wheels then it's still easy to remove them. Photo: istock

Punctures can be repaired at the side of a road or trail in a minutes. Fitting a spare innertube is quicker. Photo: Dan Joyce

time. With a quick release, tighten the knurled nut and then close the quick release lever fully. There should be some resistance when you close the lever, enough that it takes a firm hand and leaves a temporary imprint on your palm from the lever. You can undo the lever and tighten or loosen the knurled nut if there's not enough or too much resistance.

To refit the rear wheel, you also need to get the chain onto the smallest sprocket as you put the wheel in. Pull the derailleur back out of the way and move the sprockets past the top run of chain – it's the bottom run of chain,

of course, but the bike is upside down – and engage the smallest sprocket with the lower run of chain as you slot the wheel into the drop-outs. The rest is the same as for the front wheel.

PUNCTURES

First remove the wheel. Starting opposite the valve, slide a tyre lever under the wire bead in the edge of the tyre and lever it over the rim. Hook the lever to a spoke. Repeat with a second tyre lever about six inches from the first. Using a third tyre lever – or your first if you have only two – hook it under the edge of the tyre several inches further on and then slide it around to peel the tyre off the rim all the way round on one side.

Before you can pull the innertube out of the tyre, you need to free the valve from the valve hole. Remove the valve cap, and possibly a knurled lockring if it's a Presta valve, and carefully push the valve through. Now get the innertube out.

Pump up the innertube until it's twice as fat as the tyre or until you hear hissing, whichever comes first. Turn the tube past your ear to hear air escaping. If you can't hear anything, try passing the tube in front of your lips to feel the air. Submerging the tyre under water to see bubbles is a last resort. If you use it, remember to dry the tyre afterwards.

When you've found the hole, mark it with a big cross using a ballpoint pen. Hold the innertube next to the wheel, lining up the valve with the valve hole, and then check the tyre for sharps where the innertube's hole is. Turn the tube 180 degrees, keeping the valve aligned with the hole, if you can't remember which way it came out of the tyre.

Deflate the innertube. Then stretch the tube over your saddle or your fist while holding it, ballpoint pen cross uppermost, and gently roughen the tube with the sandpaper from your puncture kit. Apply *one* layer of glue in an area much bigger than the patch you're about to use, spreading it around with your finger.

Don't apply the patch yet. Hang the tube up and leave it for five minutes.

Make a cup of tea. One other job you can do is to run your fingers carefully around the inside circumference of the tyre to double-check for sharps.

When five minutes is up, peel the foil backing off a patch and apply it to the tube. Hold it down firmly, then leave it another couple of minutes. Then peel off the transparent film on the top of the patch, taking care not to lift up the patch at the edges.

If you have some talc or dust to hand, lightly dust over the spare glue that surrounds the patch. Inflate the tube a little, just enough to give it shape. Insert the valve through the valve hole and feed the rest of the

Feed your repaired or spare innertube back into the tyre. Check that one side of the tyre is still sitting on the rim, then lever the other side back in place using fingers and thumbs. It's more a matter of technique than brute strength. Photo: istock

tube into the tyre. Make sure the other edge of the tyre is still on the rim, pushing it down into the rim where necessary.

Now you can fit the other edge of the tyre, levering tyre and innertube back into the rim at the same time. Start opposite the valve. That way there's more slack in the innertube and it will be easier to lever on the tyre. Avoid using tyre levers if possible as they can pinch the tube and create another hole. Lever it on using your thumbs and fingers. This takes some strength, but it's mostly a matter of technique. Work your way around the tyre until you get to the final tight bit. If you can't push it on with your thumbs, grab the tyre in both hands from the other side and pull it on by tilting your wrists down. No joy? Let a bit more air out of the tube. Lubrication with a light dusting of talc can help tight tyres slide on, as can a water-soluble lubricant such as KY Jelly.

Two special tyre levers that can help those with a weaker grip are the VAR tyre lever (£7, www.bikeplus.co.uk) and the Crank Bros Speed Lever (£5, www.2pure.co.uk) – the latter is better at removal than fitting.

Before you re-inflate the tyre, run your hands around it and press it down into the rim to make sure it's properly 'seated'. Then pump it up again and refit the wheel – not forgetting to hook up the brake!

It's much easier to fix punctures at home than when you're out on your bike, which is why it's worth carrying a spare innertube or two. Just fit that instead, first checking the tyre thoroughly for sharps before you do so.

BRAKES AND GEARS
If brake and gear cables are too slack, they won't work properly. You need to tension the cable. The easiest way to do that is to progressively unscrew the barrel adjuster for that cable. That's found by the lever (V-brakes or mechanical disc brakes), the brake calliper (sidepull brakes) or just behind the rear derailleur. If the cable is still too slack, or there is no barrel adjuster, you'll need to undo the bolt where the cable is clamped – which is always on the brake or derailleur – pull some more cable through and re-clamp it.

CLEANING AND OILING
To clean the bike you'll want a bucket and a collection of brushes and old rags, maybe a sponge too. Use a detergent without salt, such as car shampoo, and warm water. A garden hosepipe is useful too, although you should avoid spraying high pressure jets directly at any bearings (headset, bottom bracket, wheel axles, pedals).

To get the bike more clean more easily, spray it with a biodegradable bike cleaner. Muc-Off (£6.50 for 1 litre, www.muc-off.com) is good stuff, but there lots of others. Leave it for a few minutes, then clean it with your water and brushes. Use a water soluble degreaser on the chain.

Brushes, rags, a sponge and some soapy water are all you need for cleaning – but bike cleaner helps. Photo: Dan Joyce

You can buy bike-specific brush kits and scrapers or use a combination of tooth-, scrubbing- and bottle-brushes, with screwdrivers for scraping. Clip-on chain cleaners are also available, but a couple of nail brushes clamped in one hand over the chain works just as well. Do the muckiest jobs first.

When you've finished, rinse the bike with cold water and let it drip dry(ish). After using a PTFE or water displacement spray on the chain, oil it. 'Dry' lubes are fine for bikes used on road in the summer. For bikes used off-road in Britain or in the wet, a stickier 'wet lube' is better. Apply to each link. After giving it time to soak in, wipe off any excess. Take care to avoid getting lubricants on rims or disc brake rotors.

You will also need to lubricate brake and gear pivot points – a drop or two of light oil is all it takes to keep them running smoothly. Bare cables need to be lubricated where they enter cable housing. Shift the chain onto the smallest sprocket and chainring and unhook the brakes so all cables are as slack as they can be.

Pull the cable housing away from the cable stop along the line of the frame tube and then away from the frame, letting the bare wire slot through the gap in the cable stop. Squirt a bit of PTFE into the cable housing end, then put it back in the cable stop.

ESSENTIAL TOOLKIT

Your 'on the bike' tools can do double duty as home workshop tools to begin with.

Must have
· Hand pump (e.g. Topeak Morph, £25+, www.extrauk.co.uk)
· Puncture kit with tyre levers (Rema Tip Top TT05, £4, www.ultimatepursuits.co.uk)
· Allen keys (on a multi-tool such as a Crank Bros Multi 17, £19, www.2pure.co.uk)
· Phillips head screwdriver (there's one on most multi-tools)
· 6in or 8in adjustable spanner (get a good one, such as Bahco or Draper)
· Oil and spray lube

Good to have
· Floor pump (e.g. SKS Airworx, £25, www.chickencycles.co.uk)
· Chain tool (on many multi-tools)
· Spoke keys (ditto)
· Electrical insulation tape and cable ties

Workshop tools such as a crank extractor, cable cutters and a workstand can wait.

BE SAFE **BE SEEN**

 SELF ILLUMINATING
No need to rely on external light sources

 HIGHLY VISIBLE UP TO 800M

 VISIBLE FROM ALL ANGLES

 USEABLE IN EXTREME WEATHER CONDITIONS

 3 MODES – Constant ON / Slow Blink / Fast Blink

 ADJUSTABLE FOR THE PERFECT FIT

 LIGHTWEIGHT

 EXELITE
ILLUMINATED PERSONAL SAFETY SYSTEMS
www.exelite.co.uk

Resources

CTC

CTC (the Cycling Tourists' Club) is the UK's national cyclists' organisation, with around 70,000 members and affiliates. Regardless of your age or ability, CTC is your essential cycling accessory. Benefits include:
• Free £10 million third-party insurance and legal advice
• An award-winning bi-monthly magazine, *Cycle*
• Route and touring information
• Cyclists' helpline offering advice on all cycling matters
• Campaigning on behalf of cyclists' rights
• Local groups for you to ride with
• Discounts on accommodation, accessories and travel
• Access to CTC cycling holidays and tours

Membership costs from just £12 per year. CTC has been protecting and promoting the rights of cyclists since 1878. CTC is a not-for-profit organisation that is funded through its membership and donations in return for support. To become a member, visit www.ctc.org.uk/join or phone 0870 873 0061.

FURTHER READING

Here's a selection of books to inform and inspire various members of any cycling family.

UTILITY CYCLING

Cyclecraft by John Franklin
(£12, www.cyclecraft.co.uk)
Effectively the cyclist's Highway Code and Advanced Driving instruction rolled into one.
City Cycling by Richard Ballantine
(£10, www.citycycling.org)
Pacy and upbeat guide to being a town and city cyclist.

TOURING & TRAVEL

Traffic-Free Cycle Trails by Nick Cotton
(£13, www.sustransshop.co.uk)
More than 400 rides on railway paths, towpaths, forest tracks etc.
Adventure Cycle-Touring Handbook by Stephen Lord (£14, www.trailblazer-guides.com)
Better for world travellers than family travellers, but has some good general information on touring all the same.

MOUNTAIN BIKING

Where to Mountain Bike in Britain by Nicky Crowther (£12, www.wheretomtb.com)
Covers off-road hotspots and trail centres right across the country.
The Mountain Bike Book by Steve Worland
(£20, www.haynes.co.uk)
Wide-ranging coverage of mountain biking suitable for new and returnee cyclists.

TECHNICAL

Big Blue Book of Bicycle Repair by Calvin Jones/ Park Tool (£18, www.ctcshop.com)
Step-by-step bike fixing instruction manual that's up to date with current technology
Haynes The Bike Book by Fred Milsom

(£15, www.haynes.co.uk)
Easy to understand maintenance guide that suited to beginners.
Bicycle Design by Mike Burrows
(£10, www.snowbooks.com)
Under the skin of cycle technology from an irreverent engineer.

GENERAL

Richard's 21st Century Bicycle Book by Richard Ballantine (£18, www.panmacmillan.com)
Inspirational and informed overview of the whole world of cycling.
The Cyclist's Companion by George Theohari
(£10, www.think-books.com)
Hundreds of snippets and factoids for cycling enthusiasts of any age.

HUMOUR

French Revolutions by Tim Moore
(£7, www.randomhouse.co.uk)
Very funny account of one man's attempt to ride the route of the Tour de France.
Crap Cycle Lanes by Warrington Cycle Campaign
(£5, www.eye-books.com)
The 50 worst cycle lanes in Britain, from the daft to the ridiculous.

VIDEOS AND GAMES

Roam by The Collective (£20, www.ctcshop.com and www.thecollectivefilm.com)
Beautifully shot short mountain biking film that will appeal to teens.
Downhill Domination
(£10, www.codemasters.co.uk)
12+ rated PlayStation 2 mountain bike downhill racing game in the style of *SSX*.

Glossary

700C. Roughly 27-inch diameter wheel size used for most road bikes, touring bikes and hybrids. Also used on some mountain bikes, called 29ers.

Aluminium alloy. Lightweight metal used for quality, mass-market bicycle frames and components. Fatter tubes and chunkier designs are required to optimise strength and stiffness.

Bearings. Ball bearings are used in a bike's headset, bottom bracket, hubs, pedal axles and freewheel. They may be loose, held in a circular cage, or sealed in a cartridge.

Bottom bracket. The axle that the pedal cranks are connected to at the junction of the down-tube, seat-tube and chain-stays.

Butted tube. A frame tube that has internally thicker tube walls at one end so it can be brazed or welded there without compromising its strength. A double-butted tube is thicker at both ends.

Brake blocks. Also known as brake pads. Softer pads brake more effectively but wear out faster.

Braze-ons. Non-structural frame fitments such as bottle mounts or mudguard eyelets. Often welded rather than brazed in place.

Cable housing. Bicycle gears and most brakes use Bowden cables, with a steel wire inside a steel-and-plastic outer: the cable housing.

Cable stop. Small socketed braze-on for the transition between a curved Bowden cable and a straight bare cable. Cable guides are loops for full-length Bowden cables.

Cadence. This is the pedalling speed in revolutions per minute.

Cantilever brake. Rim brake using brazed-on frame/fork pivots and a straddle cable. Used on touring, cyclo-cross and old mountain bikes.

Carbon fibre. A moulded, composite material made from a weave of carbon fibres and an epoxy resin. Excellent strength-to-weight ratio.

Cassette. Cluster of 8, 9 or 10 sprockets that slides onto a freehub.

Chain-case. Guard that fully encloses the chain.

Chain-stays. Twin frame tubes that join the rear drop-outs to the bottom bracket.

Chainring. Large cog connected to the cranks that drives the chain. Often one of two or three.

Chainset. The cranks and attached chainrings. Also known as the crankset.

Cleat. Metal or plastic shoe plate that clips into the sprung binding of a matching clipless pedal.

Clipless pedal. Confusingly named clip-in pedal that accommodates a matching cleat rather like ski bindings.

Contact points. Handlebar grips, saddle and pedals.

Cranks. Levers that connect the pedals to the chainrings.

Damping. Adjustable or fixed restriction on the rebound of a compressed suspension spring. Undamped springs bounce like pogo sticks.

Derailleur. Parallelogram mechanism that derails the chain sideways from one chainring or sprocket to another.

Disc brake. Motorcycle-style brake in which a calliper on the fork or seat-stay squeezes pistons onto a hub-mounted rotor. Some are hydraulic, others mechanical.

Down-tube. Frame tube that runs diagonally between the head-tube and the bottom bracket.

Drivetrain. The bicycle's mechanical propulsion system: pedals, chainset, bottom bracket, chain, rear sprockets, and rear hub. Also known as the transmission.

Drop bars. Hook shaped handlebar used on touring bikes, road bikes and cyclo-cross bikes that offers a variety of hand-grip positions.

Drop-outs. The slots in the fork and frame that hold the front and rear wheels.

Drum brake. An enclosed hub brake in which the pads press on the inside of a metal shell.

Eyelets. Threaded mounts for bolting on accessories such as mudguards.

Fixed wheel. A single-speed bicycle with no freewheel. When the rear wheel turns, the cranks turn too. Also called fixed gear.

Fork. The steerable front end of a cycle, connected via the steerer tube (which runs through the head-tube) to the stem and handlebar.

Frame angles. Usually refers only to the angle of the head-tube and seat-tube, which influence steering characteristics and weight distribution.

Freehub. Splined rear hub with an integral freewheel, onto which you then slot a cassette of sprockets.

Freewheel. Internal ratchet-and-pawls mechanism that transmits drive but allows you to coast without pedalling. Integral to the screw-on sprocket(s) in threaded hubs or to the hub itself in Freehubs.

Full suspension. Bike with suspension at both front and rear.

Gear range. The difference between top and bottom gear. For example, in top gear one revolution of the cranks might rotate the rear wheel four times, whereas in bottom gear one

Glossary

rotation of the cranks might rotate the rear wheel just once.

Groupset. Often taken to mean the gear shifters, derailleurs and chainset. Also includes the hubs, cassette and brakes.

Hardtail. Mountain bike with front but not rear suspension.

Headset. Bearings in the top of and bottom of the head-tube, which allow the steerer tube inside to turn. May be threaded (where the top headset race screws onto threads on the steerer to hold it in place) or, more commonly, threadless (the steerer is secured by an internal nut and bolt).

Head-tube. Short frame tube at the junction of the down- and top-tubes that holds the fork.

Hub gear. A hub with an internal 'gear box' and just one external sprocket rather than several.

Hybrid. A cross between a road or touring bike and a mountain bike. The default bike from which specialist bikes diverge.

Mech. Short for 'gear mechanism', which is the same as a derailleur.

Pannier. Bag that fits to the side of a carrier rack on the front or back of the bike.

Presta valve. Narrow valve used on road and touring bikes and high-end mountain bikes.

Quick-release. A cam-operated clamp with a lever on one end and a knurled nut on the other. Often used to hold wheels and seat-posts in place.

Recumbent. A cycle with a reclining or semi-reclining seat, ridden with the feet out in front.

Rigid. A mountain bike without suspension.

Schrader valve. Car-tyre type valve.

Seat-post. Also known as the seat-pin. The pillar that holds the saddle. Can be moved up and down in the seat-tube by loosening the seat-binder bolt.

Seat-stays. Twin frame tubes that join the rear drop-outs to the junction of the seat- and top-tubes. This can be either separate tubes or a forked wishbone.

Seat-tube. The central, near vertical frame tube that runs between the bottom bracket and the top-tube/seat-stay junction.

Shifter. Gear lever. Can be a thumb lever, two buttons, a rotary grip-shift, or else integrated with the brake lever.

Side-pull brake. Rim brake that attaches via a hole in the fork crown or seat-stay bridge. Used on road bikes and some hybrids, and can be single or dual pivot. Reach (or 'drop') for side-pull brakes is the distance between the central bolt and lowest brake block position. A longer reach is needed to clear bigger tyres and/or mudguards.

Singletrack. Usually refers to an off-road trail that's so narrow bikes have to travel in single file. Can also refer to roads where cars do the same.

Speed. When preceded by a number it refers to the number of gears, hence 8-speed, 24-speed, etc.

Sprocket. The cog or cogs on the rear hub. The number of teeth on the sprocket gives its size, so 32T is twice as big as 16T.

Steel alloy. Bikes can be made from mild-steel or high-tensile steel ('hi ten'); they're strong but very heavy. Steel alloys such as chrome-molybdenum ('cro-mo') have a better strength-to-weight ratio.

Stem. Joins the handlebar to the steerer tube. A threadless stem clamps the outside of the steerer. A quill stem uses a wedge bolt on the inside of the steerer, and requires a threaded headset.

Steerer tube. The top part of the fork, which passes through the head tube and is clamped by the stem.

Stiffness. A frame or component's resistance to being temporarily deformed (i.e. flexed).

Strength. A frame or component's resistance to being permanently deformed (i.e. broken).

Suspension. All bikes have some suspension courtesy of pneumatic tyres. So suspension is usually taken to mean additional suspension, from springs in the fork or frame.

Toe overlap. Where your foot on the pedal can hit the front wheel during a turn.

Top-tube. The sloped or horizontal upper frame tube that joins the head-tube to the seat-tube. 'Open frame' bikes don't have a top-tube.

Track pump. A floor pump with a large barrel, a two-handed handle, and a long tube for the pump-head.

Transmission. The drivetrain.

Tyre size. The nomenclature is confusing. A 29-inch tyre is the same as a 28-inch tyre and a 700C tyre! Use the ISO numbers printed on the sidewall, which give tyre width followed by diameter at the rim in millimetres.

V-brake. A direct-pull cantilever brake with longer brake arms and more mechanical advantage than traditional cantilevers. Uses the same frame studs but requires dedicated brake levers.

Wheelbase. The distance between the wheel axles. A longer wheelbase gives steadier or slower steering.

Woods valve. A third valve type sometimes found on old or Continental bikes. You can inflate it with a Presta pump.

cycle

The Magazine of the National Cyclists' Association

& The UK's Highest Circulating Cycle Magazine

Published Bi – Monthly

To Receive your FREE copy every issue become a
CTC Member, call 0870 873 0065
write: CTC, P.O. Box 510, Unit 8, Isleworth, TW7 6WP
or E-Mail: membership@ctc.org.uk

Index